KNOWLEDGE ENCYCLOPEDIA
HUMAN BODY
IMMUNE SYSTEM AND COMMON DISEASES

© Wonder House Books 2024

All rights reserved. No part of this book may be reproduced or transmitted in any form by any means, electronic or mechanical, including photocopying and recording, or by any information storage and retrieval system except as may be expressly permitted in writing by the publisher.

Wonder House
(An imprint of Prakash Books)

contact@wonderhousebooks.com

Disclaimer: The information contained in this encyclopedia has been collated with inputs from subject experts. All information contained herein is true to the best of the Publisher's knowledge.

ISBN : 9789389931235

Table of Contents

Our Body's Army	3
Our Skin: The Great Wall	4–5
The Organs that Protect Us	6–7
Immune Cells: Tireless Soldiers	8–9
Phagocytosis: Eating Our Body's Enemies	10
Shoot at Sight	11
You are Under Attack	12–13
Clotting and Wound Healing	14
Platelets: Our Body's Repairmen	15
Keeping Our Gut and Lungs Safe	16
Our Microscopic Allies	17
How Our Immune System Fights	18–19
Our Immune System's Chemical Toolkit	20–21
Our Soldiers Never Forget	22
Why We Get Allergies	23
Fighting Cancer	24
When Our Soldiers Turn Against Us	25
Fighting Common Diseases	26–27
Vaccines: A Jab of Safety	28–29
Immunity in Plants & Animals	30
Helping Our Immune System	31
Word Check	32

OUR BODY'S ARMY

If there were no bacteria, fungi or viruses in the world, we would not need an immune system. But since they exist and (some) even cause diseases in our body, we need ways to defend ourselves. Just as a country has police officers to safeguard against troublemakers, the body too has a complex immune system that protects it from diseases.

Our immune system is always working to keep us safe, whether we are pricked by a needle or affected by a very serious disease. The skin is the first line of defence in our body. Our body has organs where immune cells are 'trained' to fight, just like the police is trained to fight. The immune system is a master of disguise—it has special cells that work like spies, travelling around the body, looking for any invaders.

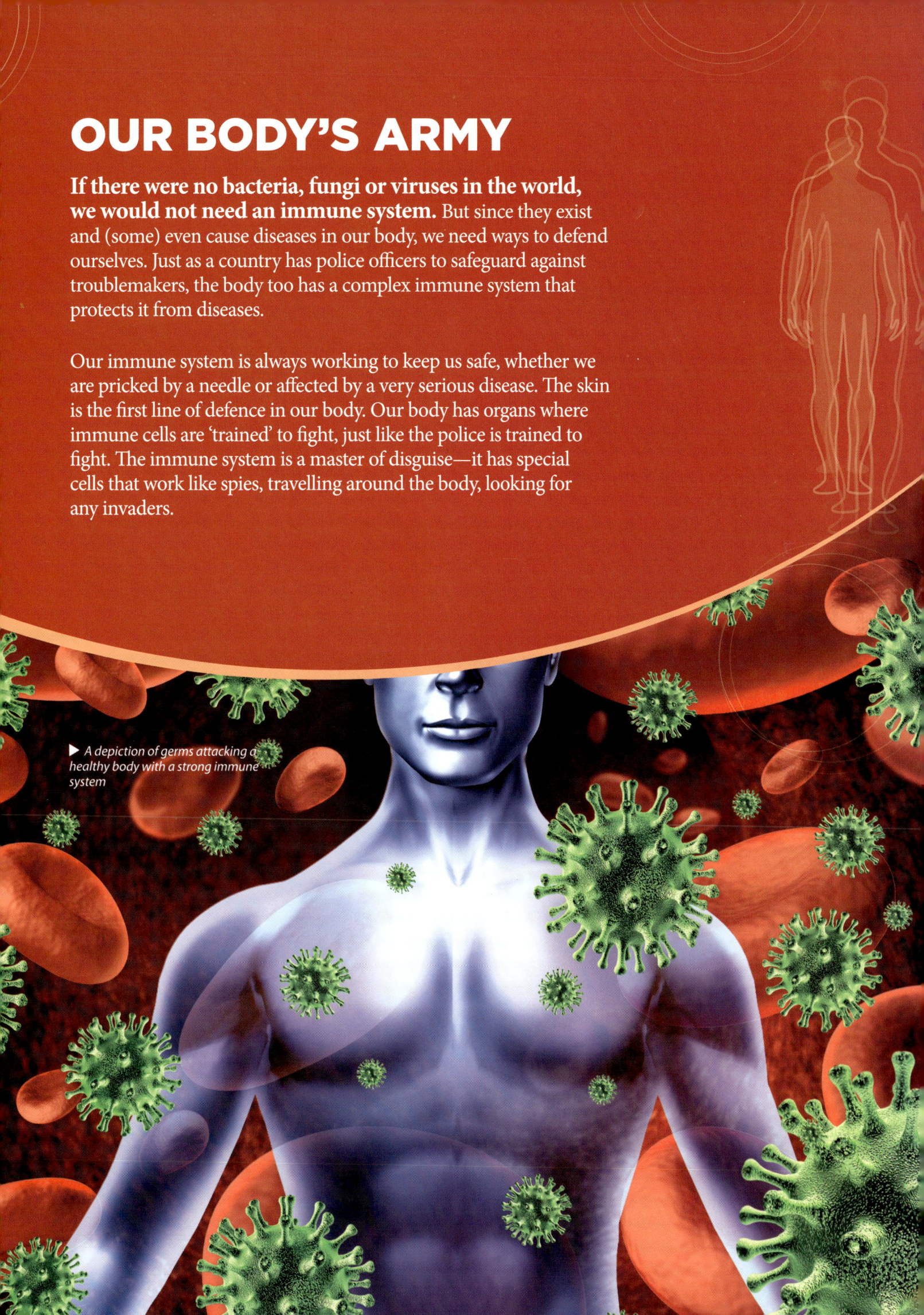

▶ A depiction of germs attacking a healthy body with a strong immune system

Our Skin: The Great Wall

Did you know that the largest organ of the body is your skin? It is the first defender of the body. It keeps the internal organs safe from the ill effects of varying temperatures. Our skin is made up of three layers—while the outermost layer is called the **epidermis**, the inner layer found beneath the epidermis is known as **dermis**. It contains hair follicles, sweat glands and connective tissue. The third layer is the **hypodermis**, a deeper subcutaneous tissue which is made up of fat and connective tissue.

Your skin is also your body's first immune warning system. It can stretch and also squeeze itself. That is why your skin does not tear when you extend your arms during a stretch or crouch down to find a coin that rolled under the bed. Your skin has nerves that tell you when something has touched it.

▼ Children have thinner skin than adults. So, children absorb harmful agents faster than adults

Keratinocytes

Keratinocytes are wonder cells that perform many functions. These cells are tightly packed together to keep out foreign particles like bacteria and viruses. They make vitamin D in the presence of sunlight. Keratinocytes also make **keratin**, which is needed to form the hair and nails. They detect wounds and heal the skin. They alert the immune system to destroy particles that might have entered from an open wound.

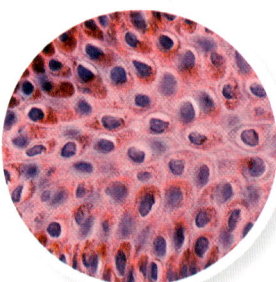

▲ Keratinocytes perform many functions

Hair Follicles

Hair follicles are the organs from where hair grows. Hair is made of fibres of a protein called keratin. The hair on our bodies is of two types—the long wiry hair which we can see and which keeps us warm by forming a carpet that traps air. When we are cold or scared, the hair stands straight. This is what is meant by 'goose bumps'. It then traps a thicker carpet of hair.

Our skin also has shorter, white hair, which cannot be seen without a magnifying lens. These act like burglar alarms. If a louse, bedbug, fly or mosquito brushes against them, they trigger the nervous system, which in turn makes us 'itch'. We scratch without even thinking ('instinct') and scrape off the creature.

In Real Life

The darker a person's skin is, the safer they are from ultraviolet (UV) rays of the Sun. That is because the darker a person is, the more melanin they have in their skin. Melanin stops 99 per cent of UV rays from entering the body and causing harmful diseases like cancer. However, no matter what the colour of your skin is, you need to apply sunscreen and protect your skin from sunburn or other damage.

The Inner Skin

In the dermis, there are **sweat glands**, oil glands, hair follicles and blood vessels. Sweat glands keep the body cool by releasing water (along with some salt and amino acids) onto the skin, which evaporates and cools it. However, if we sweat too much, a lot of amino acids collect on the skin. Bacteria can grow on these and, in turn, produce smelly chemicals. That is why when sweat collects in the armpits, it begins to smell bad.

The oil glands are also called **sebaceous glands**, because they produce an oil called **sebum**. It spreads all over our skin and makes sure that water does not enter skin from outside. That is why, even if you get wet in the rain, you do not soak up water like a sponge. Sebum also prevents bacteria and fungi from growing on the skin.

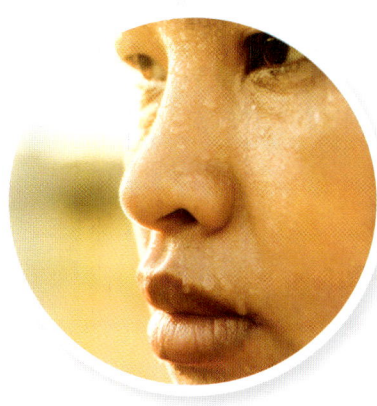

▲ Sweat prevents your body from overheating

▼ Your skin is like an onion. The outermost layers of the skin are made of dead cells, while the inner layers are made of living cells

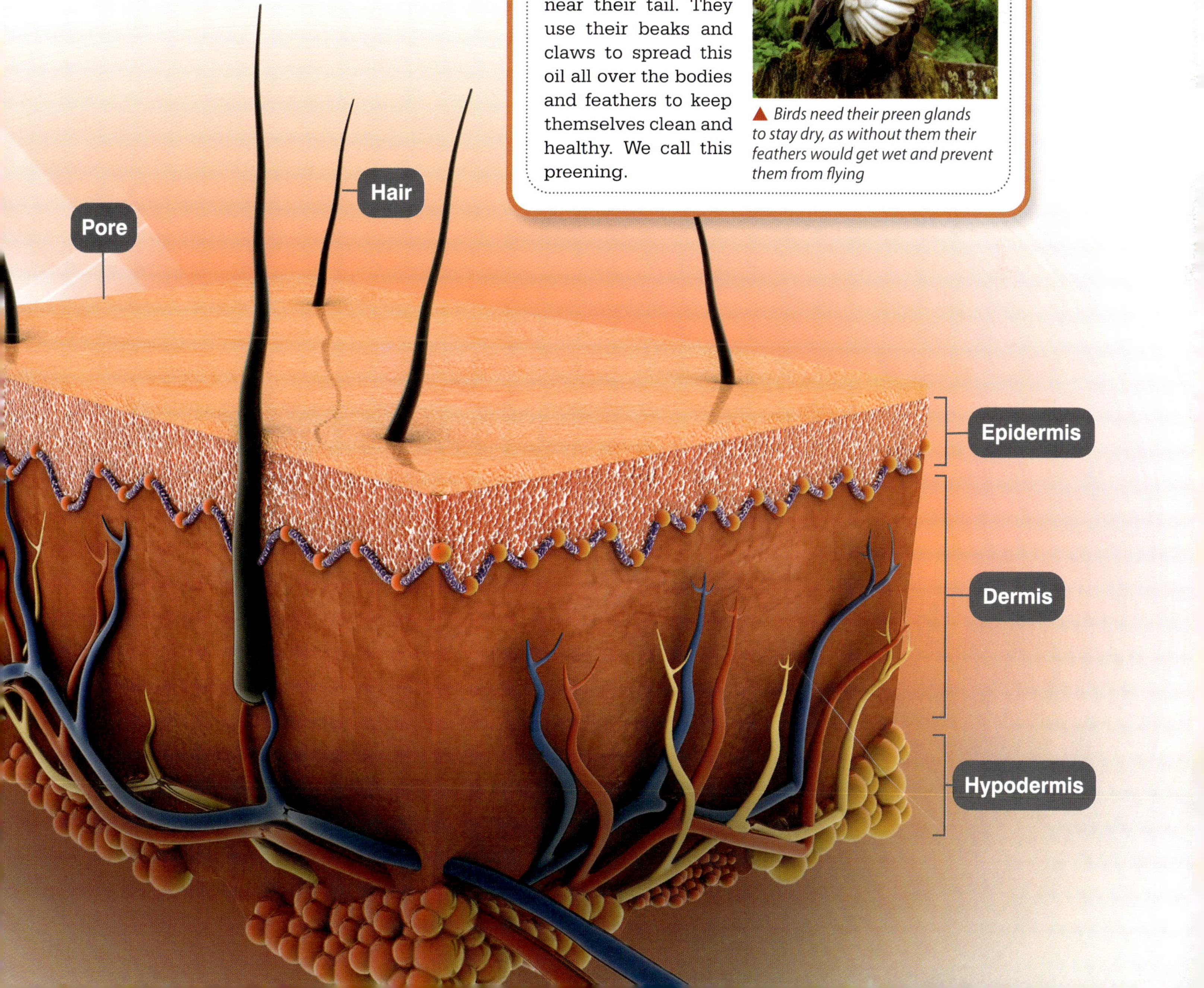

Isn't It Amazing!

Birds do not have oil glands throughout their skin, but a single 'preen gland' near their tail. They use their beaks and claws to spread this oil all over the bodies and feathers to keep themselves clean and healthy. We call this preening.

▲ Birds need their preen glands to stay dry, as without them their feathers would get wet and prevent them from flying

Pore

Hair

Epidermis

Dermis

Hypodermis

The Organs that Protect Us

Did you know that our immune system is not really a system? As the name suggests, the immune system performs the critical role of defending the body against foreign bodies, viruses, bacteria, etc. However, it may surprise you to know that the immune system is unlike the other organ systems that make up the human body. That is because it has no organs dedicated solely to itself, as is the case with the digestive system or nervous system. Instead, the organs of the immune system work towards safeguarding the body in addition to performing other functions.

Lymph Nodes

The **lymph nodes** are part of the **lymphatic system**, which is our body's second circulatory system after blood. This system carries lymph, a colourless liquid that contains the waste products of our tissues. Lymph passes through a number of tiny organs called lymph nodes, which filter the lymph and remove pathogens, broken cells, etc. Like in the spleen, these are then destroyed by the immune system.

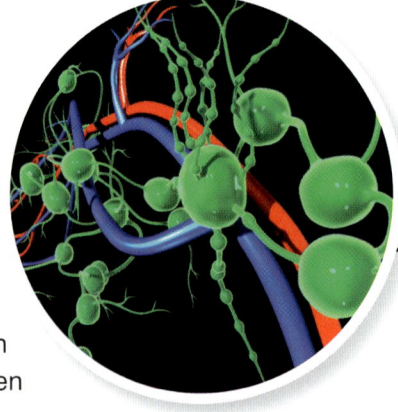
▲ *Lymph nodes filter germs and train WBCs*

The lymph nodes also act as resting camps for B- and T-cells. In an active infection, a lymph node will swell up, so that more soldier cells can come in and fight the pathogens as they are brought in by the lymph.

Bone Marrow

This is the fleshy tissue inside most large bones. This is where red blood cells (RBCs), white blood cells (WBCs) and platelets are born. Their parent cells are called stem cells. The bone marrow also trains some of the WBCs to fight disease-causing germs called **pathogens**. These trained cells are called B-cells.

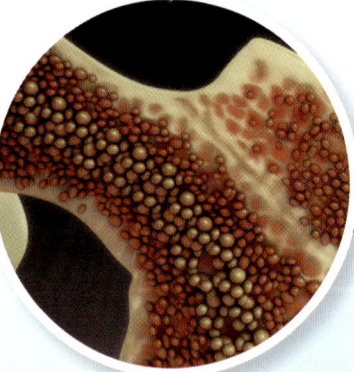
▲ *The bone marrow makes blood cells*

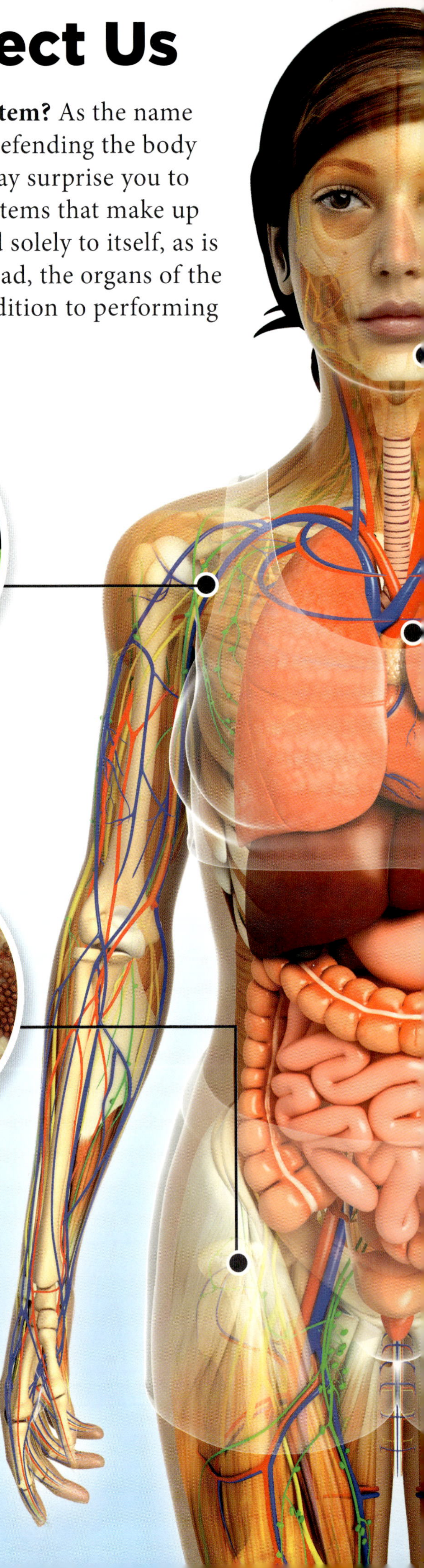

In Real Life

Some people have a defective bone marrow, and therefore they get a disease called thalassaemia. This disease causes both anaemia (lack of RBCs) and low immunity (lack of WBCs). Patients feel tired all the time, have paler skin than normal, slow growth of the body and have excess iron in their bodies. The only known cure is a transplant of bone marrow from a close relative.

HUMAN BODY — IMMUNE SYSTEM & COMMON DISEASES

◄ *The diagram shows the main organs of the immune system*

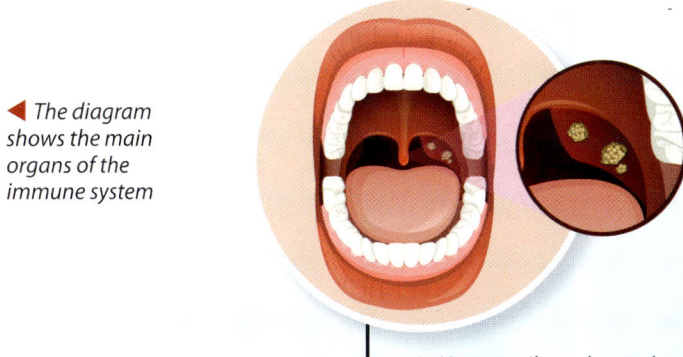

▲ *Your tonsils are located at the end of your mouth*

Tonsils and Adenoids

These are the lymph nodes that are present in our throat. They help to fight off infections in our mouth and nose respectively. Like all lymph nodes, they swell up during an infection. Unfortunately, this swelling can cause problems with swallowing food or breathing. That is why you have to have your tonsils removed if they swell up too much. The swelling of adenoids causes snoring, because they block the passage of air from the nose into the lungs.

Thymus

The thymus is a tiny organ between the heart and the breastbone. It performs many tasks for the body, including training a class of WBCs called T-cells. The thymus also acts as a resting camp for other kinds of WBCs.

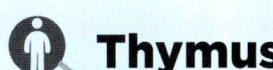

▲ *The thymus trains WBCs to recognise germs*

Spleen

The spleen is a tiny organ near your stomach. It is a resting place for platelets, though its main job is to break the worn-out RBCs. It acts like a filter where the good RBCs are separated from damaged RBCs and platelets, pathogens and other stuff. The spleen needs phagocytes (see pp 8–9) to attack RBCs and destroy them.

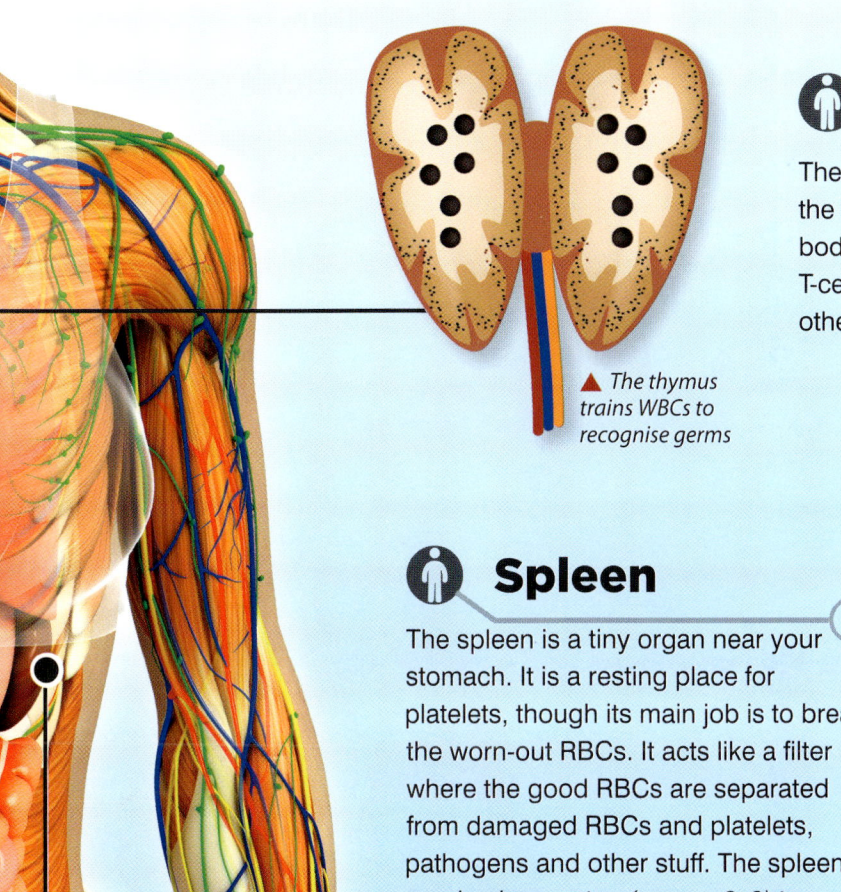

◄ *The spleen filters blood, kills dead RBCs and acts as a training ground for WBCs*

Isn't It Amazing!

Ever squashed a mosquito and seen a splat of red blood? That is your own blood! Insects have no blood, they only have lymph, which drains out the body's waste and has cells to fight pathogens. Blood only developed with the evolution of vertebrates, which includes human beings, as well as other mammals, fish, amphibians, reptiles and birds.

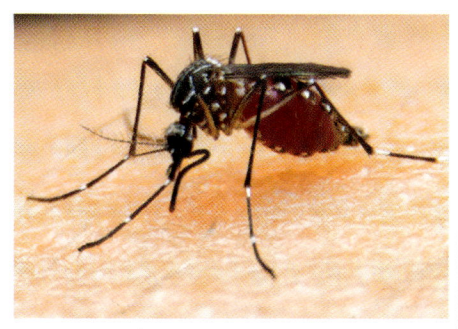

▲ *A mosquito sucking blood. Note its abdomen is full of human blood. Insects have no blood, only lymph*

Immune Cells: Tireless Soldiers

An army has many kinds of soldiers. There are snipers, tank-drivers, fighter pilots, drone operators and engineers. In the same way, our body has immune cells and the cells of the immune system come in many types. These cells are together called white blood cells (WBCs). They can travel quickly to any part of the body through the blood and lymph, where they detect and destroy pathogens.

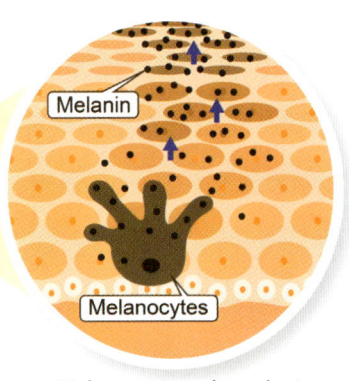

 ## Melanocytes

These cells live in the skin and produce **melanin**, which gives our skin its colour. They also act as scouts, looking for bacteria, viruses, fungi, pollen, dust, smoke particles, etc., that might have entered our body.

▲ Melanocytes make melanin

Monocytes

Monocytes are WBCs that circulate in the blood. When they get the signal that an invasion has happened, they swell up and turn themselves into lethal **macrophages**. At this stage, they leave the blood to enter the body tissues, with a mission to eliminate the harmful particles.

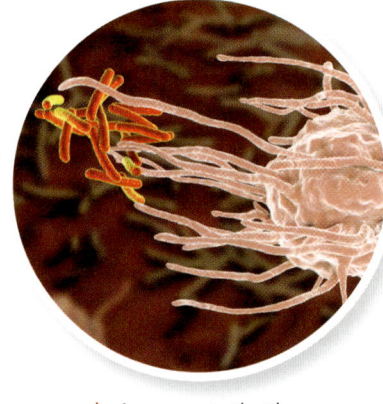

▲ A monocyte that has become a macrophage

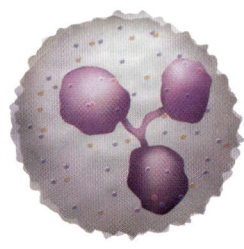

▲ Neutrophils are full of histamines and other biochemicals

 ## Neutrophils

Neutrophils are WBCs that are filled with chemicals called **histamines**. They attack the pathogen and release the histamine all over it. Histamines bring macrophages to the site, which finish the job.

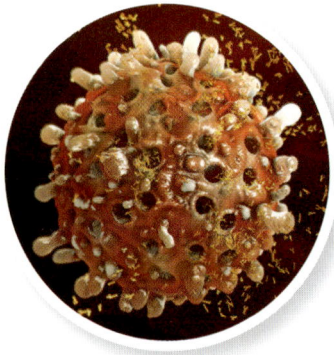

▲ B-cells are chemical weapons specialists

 ## B-cells

B-cells make a special type of protein called **antibodies**. The B-cells make thousands of different antibodies, each of which can identify a different bacteria or virus. Antibodies stick all over the pathogens and then the immune system's T-cells come and kill them.

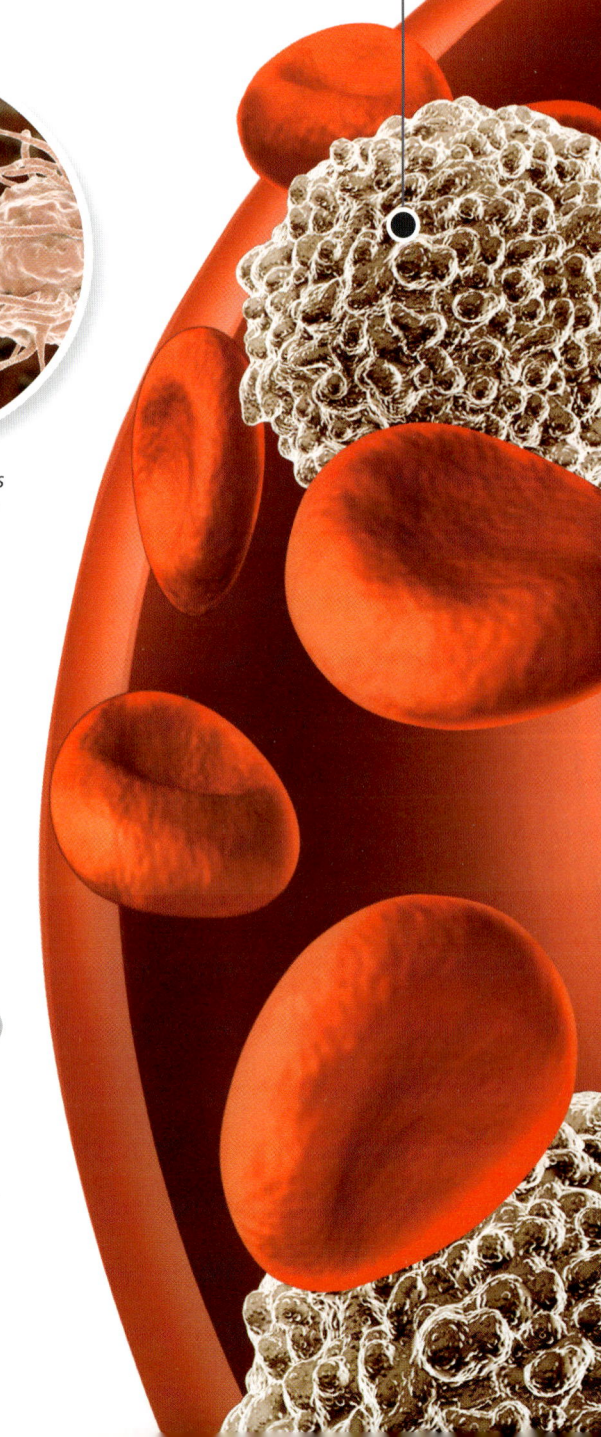

▼ White blood cells (WBCs) travel through blood to reach the infected tissue, following chemical signals

HUMAN BODY | IMMUNE SYSTEM & COMMON DISEASES

Basophils

There are not too many of these WBCs when we are healthy. But when we get bitten by an insect, or have a worm infection, they flock to the site and multiply quickly. They cause redness at the place where you got bitten, known as **inflammation**.

◄ *Basophils carry histamines and enzymes that smash up the pathogen and call for more help*

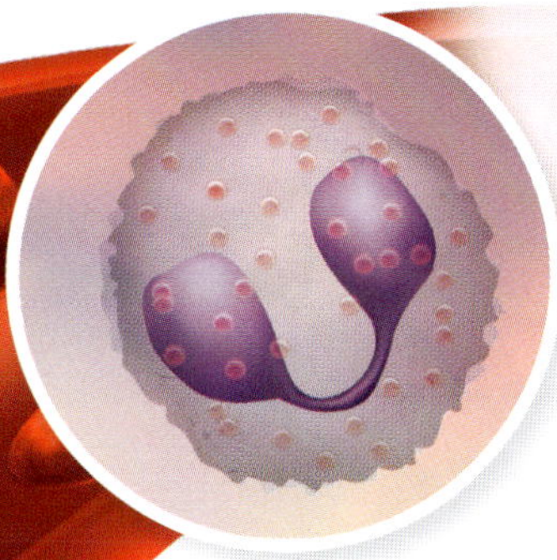

Eosinophils

Eosinophils work a lot like basophils, but they are also involved in allergies and asthma.

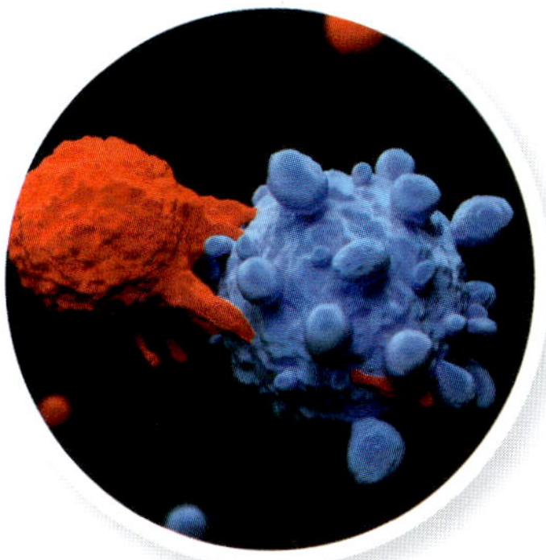

▲ *Eosinophils cells sit in the intestines and other organs that are exposed to the environment*

T-cells

T-cells are like the special forces or naval SEALs. They perform many functions such as targeting and killing cancer cells and pathogens. You will read more about these cells in detail later.

▲ *T-cells are called when the others are unable to do the job on their own*

Phagocytes

Unlike the other immune cells, phagocytes are present throughout the body. When they are present in the intestines, lungs and the lining of the nose, they are called **dendritic cells**. In the skin, there is a special type of phagocyte called **Langerhans cells**, which detect and destroy foreign invaders.

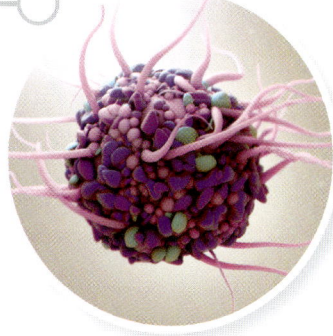

▲ *Phagocytes*

Natural Killer Cells

Natural killer cells perform the important function of finding and killing cancer cells before they take over the body.

Phagocytosis
Eating Our Body's Enemies

Phagocytosis is the body's way of getting rid of any other foreign agent that enters it. These could be bacteria, fungi or viruses. Phagocytosis is also the main immune defence of all animals, from the most primitive sponges to insects and mammals alike. In our bodies, this job is done by immune cells.

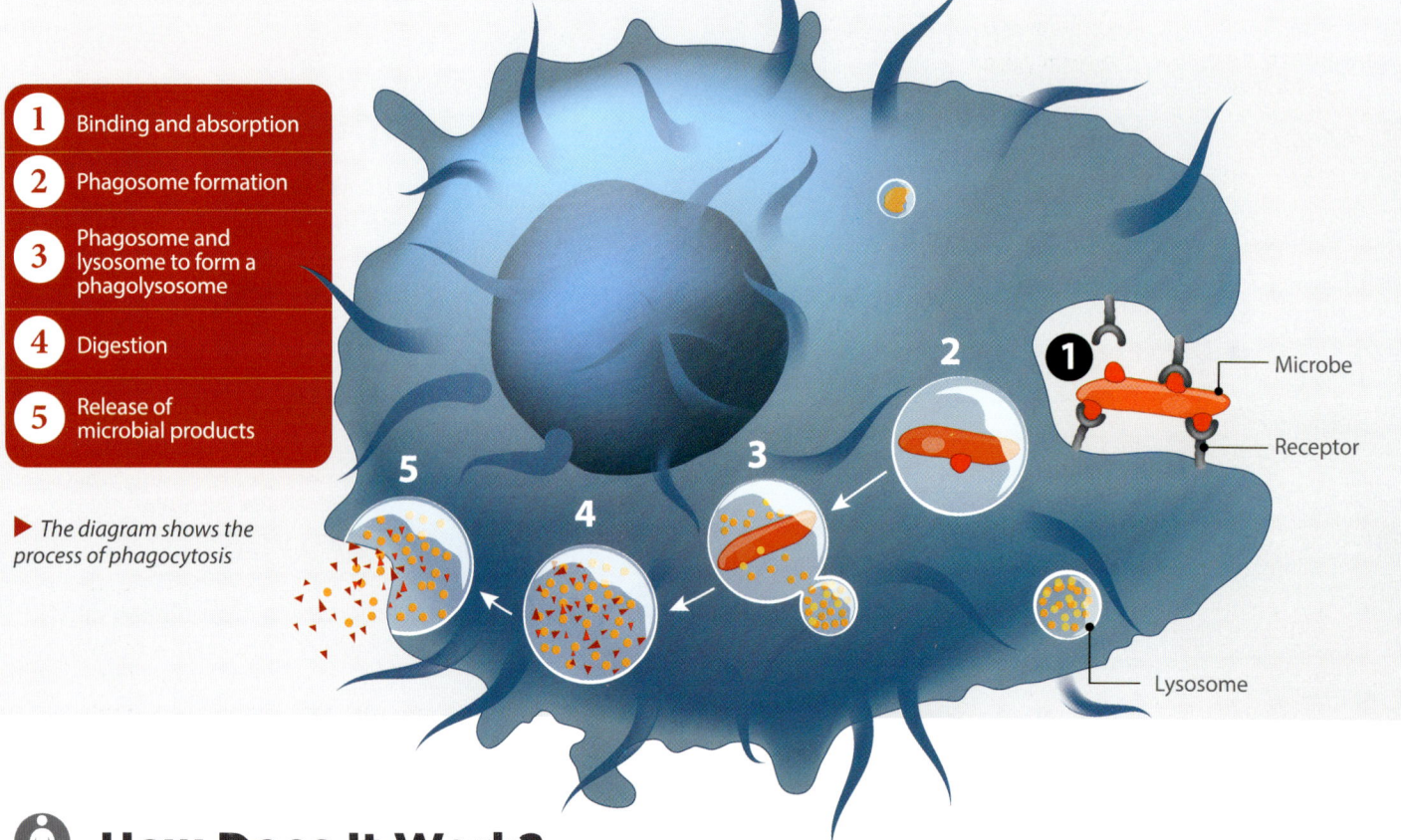

1. Binding and absorption
2. Phagosome formation
3. Phagosome and lysosome to form a phagolysosome
4. Digestion
5. Release of microbial products

▶ The diagram shows the process of phagocytosis

How Does It Work?

Phagocytosis works in a specific way. On the surface of the phagocyte cells, there are proteins called receptors that recognise a pathogen when they brush against it. Once they detect the pathogens, the cell membrane immediately surrounds the particle until it is completely enveloped or captured. It is like covering yourself with a blanket.

The ends of the membrane meet and the pathogen is captured in a **phagosome**. The cell has little bags called **lysosomes**, filled with enzymes. Lysosomes merge with phagosomes to form phagolysosomes. These phagolysosomes have enzymes that break up the proteins, carbohydrates and fats from the foreign body. Most of the broken remains are removed from the cell, and then the body, through the lymph.

Many different kinds of cells can do this. Some of the immune cells also do another job—they pick up some of the remains of the things they ate up and display them on the surface of their cell membranes, like identity tags. Other cells of the immune system use these tags to identify the kind of infection we have. These immune cells can then respond in a way that ensures the infection is cleaned out completely.

Isn't It Amazing!

Ever seen an amoeba under a microscope? Our body's WBCs behave exactly like the amoeba. They can also move on their own, especially in the spaces between cells in tissues where the blood cannot reach.

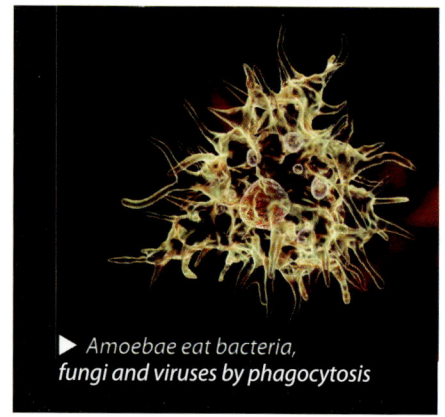

▶ Amoebae eat bacteria, fungi and viruses by phagocytosis

HUMAN BODY | IMMUNE SYSTEM & COMMON DISEASES

Shoot at Sight

There is a special way by which our body fights diseases. Each pathogen (bacteria, viruses, fungi, plasmodia and worms) is made of different kinds of proteins and other biochemicals.

Antigens

Bits of these pathogens are used by the immune system to recognise pathogens. These bits are called **antigens** and this job is done by the cells that perform phagocytosis. If the macrophages and dendritic cells are like the policemen showing the antigen, the T-cells and B-cells set out to look for the pathogen, just like a sniffer dog can identify a criminal based on a handkerchief that he has left behind at the scene of the crime. Both have different proteins on their surface that try to match the antigen. If the match is perfect, then the cells get to work.

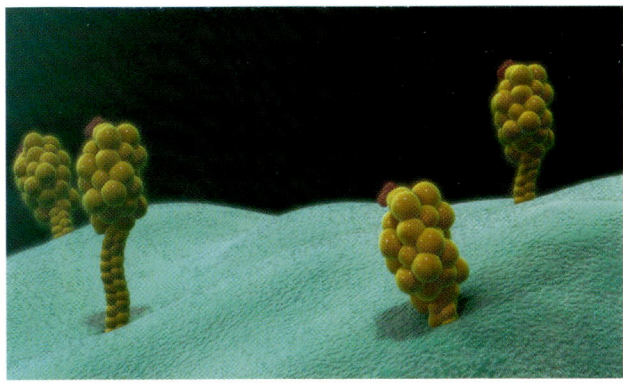

▲ *Parts of a pathogen displayed on the surface of a phagocyte that ate it. These parts are called antigens.*

◀ *The picture shows a dendritic cell that presents antigens to the (blue) T-cells to see which one matches*

In Real Life

Why do we have different blood groups? This is because the RBCs of our bodies have different antigens on their surfaces. Some people have a type called A, so they belong to Blood Group A. People of Blood Group B have another type called B. Some people have both types (thus Blood Group AB) and some have none (they are called Blood Group O).

Antibodies

Antibodies are our body's chief biochemical weapons. Antibodies are proteins made by the B-cells and each one is made to match a particular antigen. For example, if the B-cell that makes anti-chicken pox antibodies meets a cell showing the chicken pox antigen, it will make these antibodies by the thousands. The antibodies are released into the blood, where they latch on to the chicken pox viruses. Other biochemicals in the blood (called cytokines) recognise these covered viruses and get the commando cells to swallow them up.

▶ *The illustration shows antibodies attacking a virus*

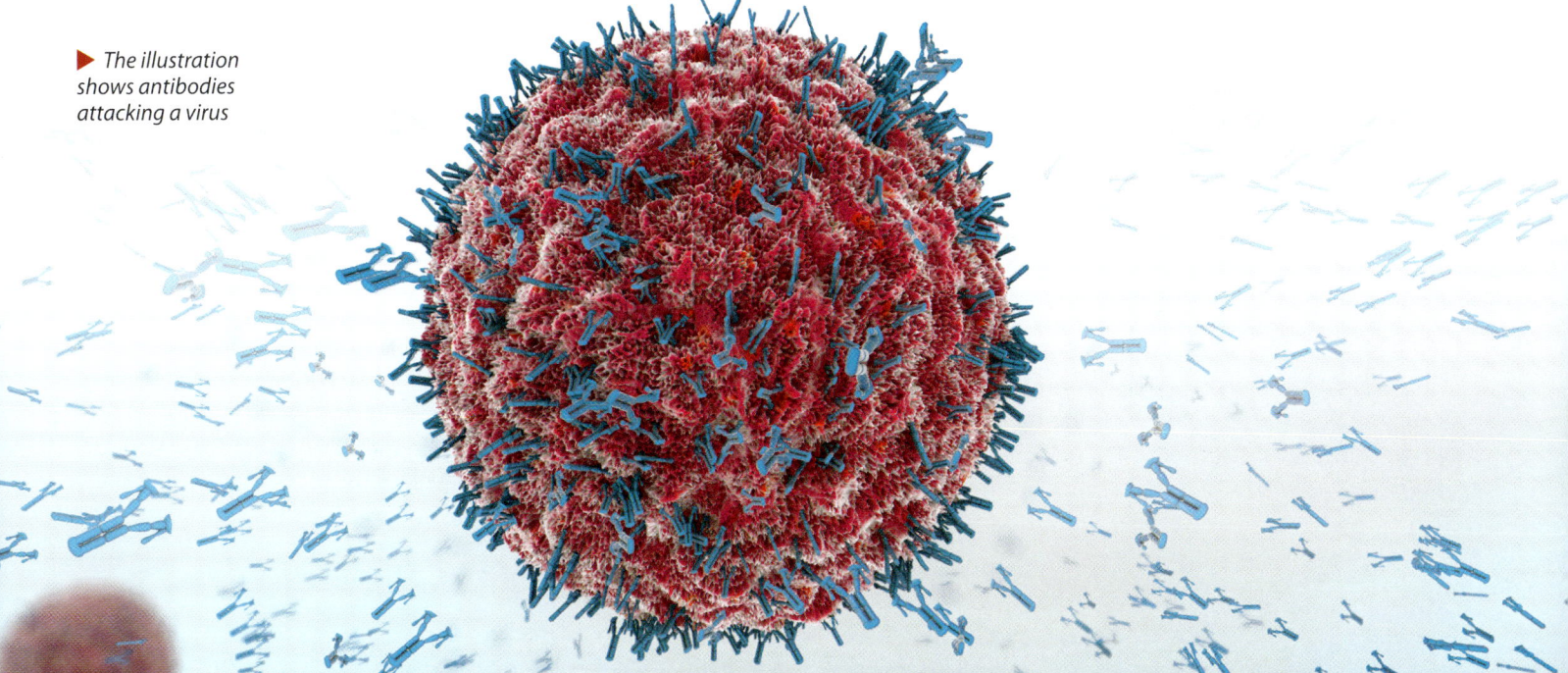

You are Under Attack

Our body can be attacked in two ways: either by pathogens or allergens. Pathogens are living creatures like viruses, bacteria, fungi, plasmodia and worms. Allergens are often non-living things like dust and certain kinds of chemicals, as well as living things like pollen, nuts, vegetables or meat products.

Pathogens

Many pathogens invade our body when our immune system is weak. Doctors call them facultative parasites. Some, like the one that causes malaria, however, must invade our bodies because they can only reproduce that way. Doctors call them obligate parasites.

There are other microscopic creatures that are called commensals. They hang around on our skins or our intestines, living off sweat and undigested food. Some of them help us fight off pathogens and make the vitamins we need.

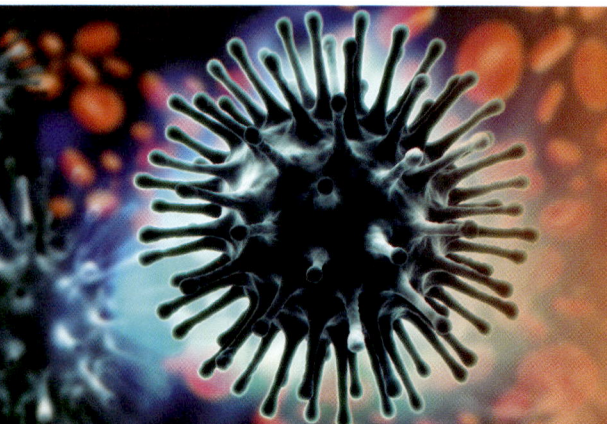

◀ Viruses hide inside human cells, so the immune system must catch them before they can get inside our cells

Viruses

Viruses are so tiny that you cannot see them with the naked eye. They are the tiniest living organisms. They are simple organisms made of DNA covered by a coat of protein—we are not even sure that they are really living things. Viruses are the cause of different kinds of diseases, from common cold to swine flu, dengue fever and even HIV/AIDS.

Fungi

Most fungi are not infectious. But those that are, infect the tongue (like white-tongue) or the skin (like ringworm). Fungal infections often happen when the immune system is weak, especially when the body is recovering from a major illness.

▶ Cells of the pathogenic fungus Candida stick to the tongue, making it look white

Bacteria

Bacteria cause most of the diseases known to us, from pimples on the skin to fevers and cholera, leprosy and tuberculosis. Bacteria are the simplest kinds of cells, with just cytoplasm covered by a cell wall.

There are two types of bacteria—those that need oxygen (obligate aerobes) and those that do not need oxygen (obligate anaerobes). *Bacillus subtilis* is an obligate aerobe. *Clostridium* is a rod-shaped bacterium found in the intestinal tracts of animals and human beings. It does not need oxygen to grow.

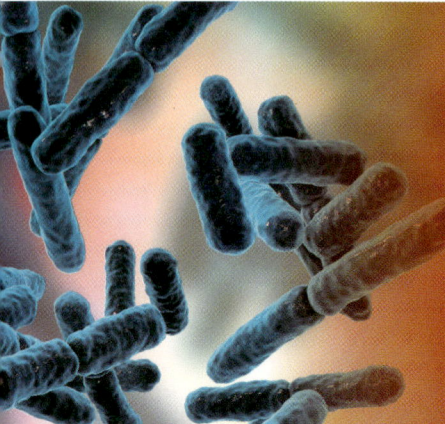

◀ Bacteria come in many sizes and shapes, from round, pea-like cocci to rod-like bacilli, spirals and threads

HUMAN BODY — IMMUNE SYSTEM & COMMON DISEASES

💡 Isn't It Amazing!

Viruses need to get inside another living thing to make more viruses. Therefore, they will infect any living thing, from human beings and other animals to plants and one-celled creatures like amoebae and even bacteria. These last ones are called **bacteriophages**.

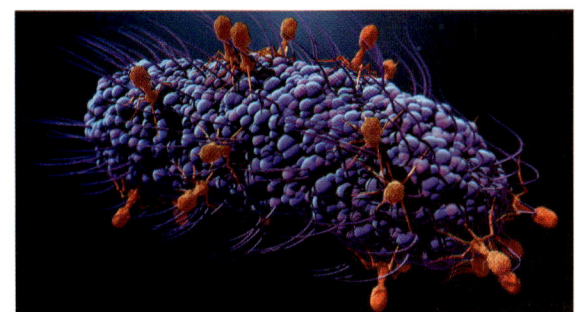

▲ Scientists are using bacteriophages to treat some infections caused by bacteria

👤 Worms

If you think of worms, you are probably thinking of earthworms. But the worms that attack human beings are really tiny, called **helminths**. The most common of these are tapeworms, which infect the intestine.

▶ Some helminths drill through the intestine wall and get into the blood, through which they can reach the brain

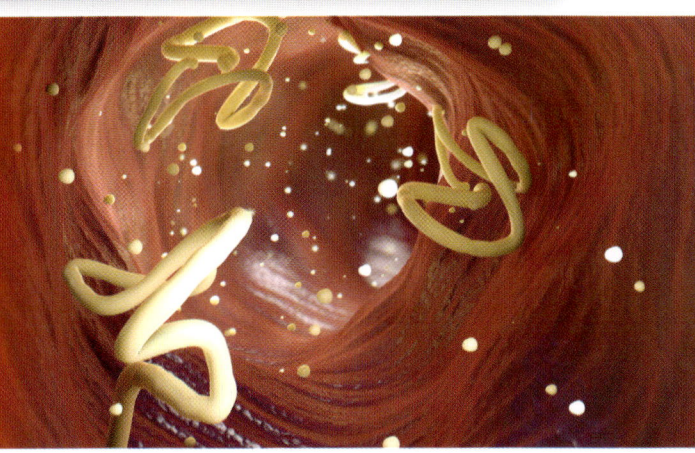

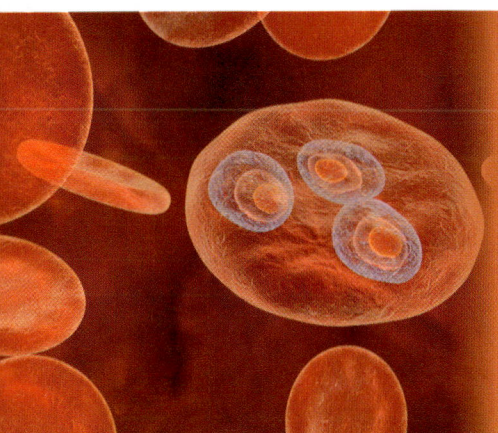

◀ Plasmodium hides inside red blood cells to escape the immune system, so it is a hard enemy to fight

👤 Protozoa

Protozoa are one-celled animals that have a nucleus and no cell wall. Protozoa cause some of the deadliest diseases known to us, like malaria, caused by Plasmodium, and sleeping sickness caused by Trypanosoma. Protozoa cannot infect us without an agent, which is often an insect that bites us, like the mosquito. The insects live in tropical regions, so the diseases they cause are called tropical diseases.

👤 Pollen

While pollen do not really attack or invade our bodies, when they are in the air, they get into our systems through breath and food. Pollen triggers the allergic response of the immune system in some people, which causes hay fever, which includes sneezing, reddening of the eyes and itching in the throat.

▶ Allergic patients need to be careful in spring, as repeated exposure to pollen can cause death

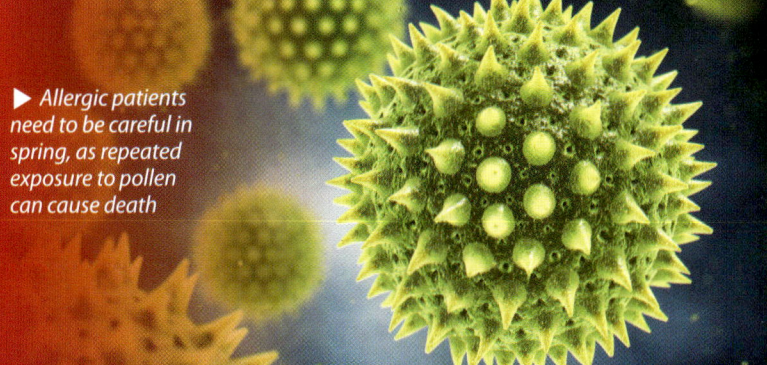

Clotting and Wound Healing

Did you ever get bruised or cut, and bleed? Did you wonder why it stopped after a while? That is because blood clots. An injury, like a cut or prick, makes a hole in your artery or vein, but the body plugs it very fast, so that you do not lose any more blood. If your blood did not clot, it would keep oozing and you would soon die.

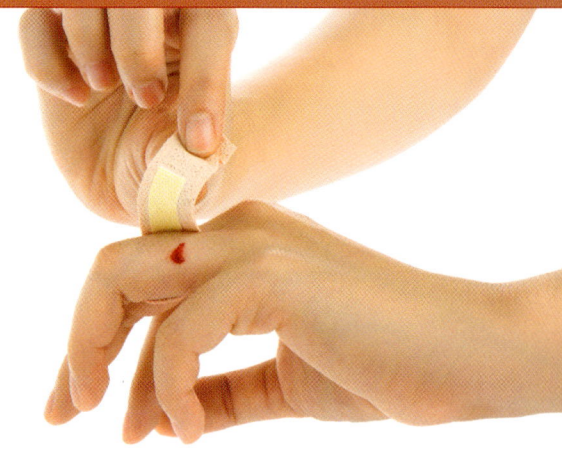

▲ Putting a band-aid on a wound helps to keep it sterile and prevents you from losing blood

Brain Clots

Blood is supplied to the brain by tiny arteries that have very thick walls. In case a clot forms in one of these, it is very hard to dislodge it.

The blood stops flowing to that part of the brain and it soon becomes starved of oxygen. If this continues for too long, the patient can get a stroke. In serious cases, it can lead to paralysis and even death. It is called haemorrhage or apoplexy.

◀ A clot is made of a big mass of fibrin threads and cells

⭐ Incredible Individuals

Some people suffer from a disease called haemophilia, in which their blood does not clot. They have to be extremely careful, as they can bleed to death even if they have a small wound. It is called the Royal Disease, because Queen Victoria's children and grandchildren suffered from it. Her son, Prince Leopold, died in 1884 at the age of 30 after he slipped and fell. He had no visible injuries but had bled internally.

◀ Prince Leopold suffered from haemophilia

How Does Blood Clot?

Platelets are the cells that carry out this process. When there is a wound, platelets stick to the tissues that get exposed because of it. They make little chemicals called amines, that get into the blood. These amines react with other chemicals that are together called the **complement pathway**.

The plasma of your blood has a protein in it called fibrinogen. When the complement pathway meets it, the fibrinogen turns into **fibrin**. Fibrin is a thread-like material that gets deposited on the cut. It soon forms a net that traps the red blood cells flowing out of the wound. After this, the skin's self-healing mechanism takes over and closes the wound over the next few days. You get a black, scaly covering called scar tissue, that often itches. Once skin has grown back, scar tissue falls away. Vitamin K is very important for clotting.

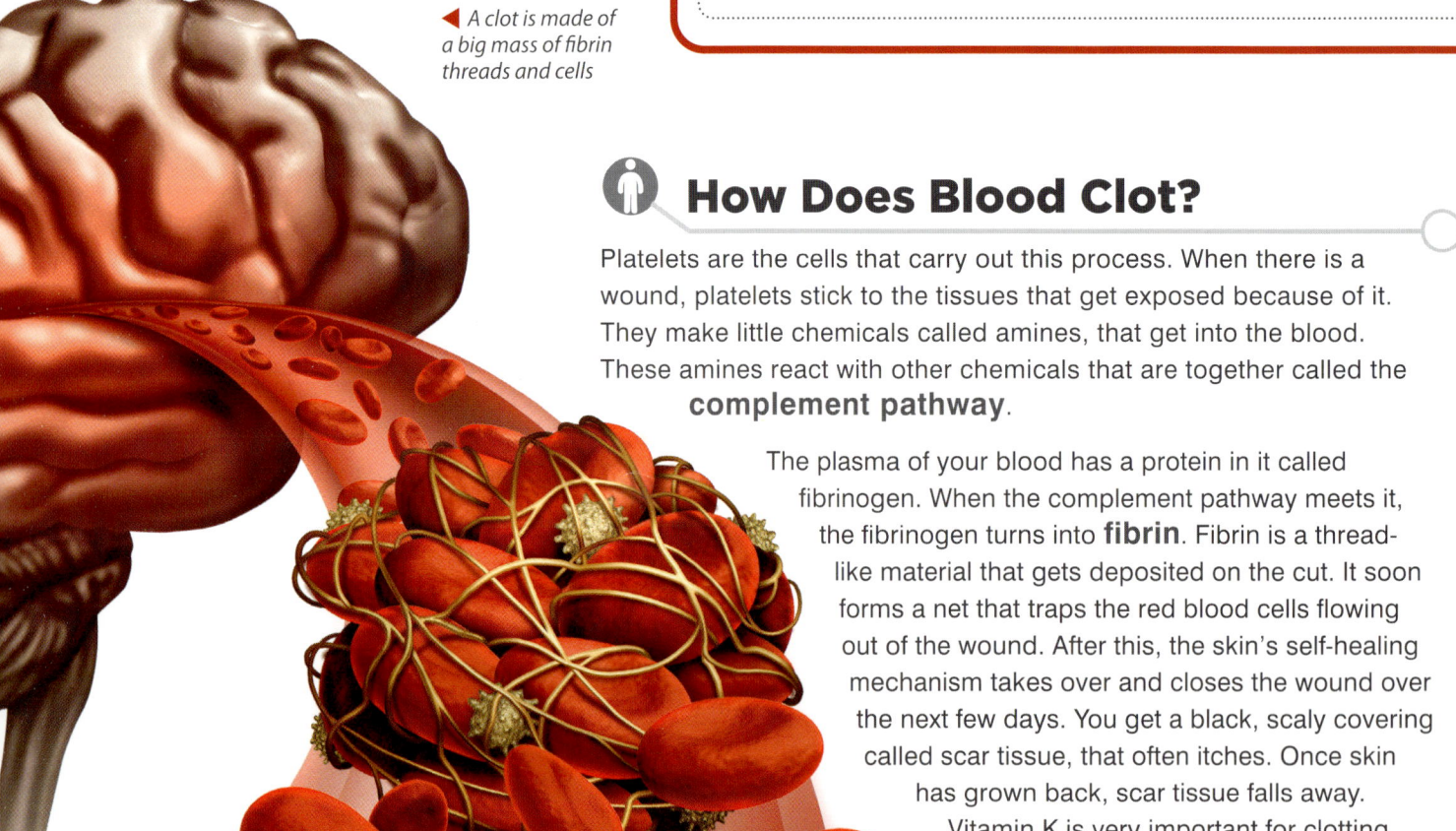

Platelets: Our Body's Repairmen

Did you know that platelets are the cells with the shortest life span in our blood? They are born in the bone marrow and live for less than 10 days, after which they die in the spleen and liver.

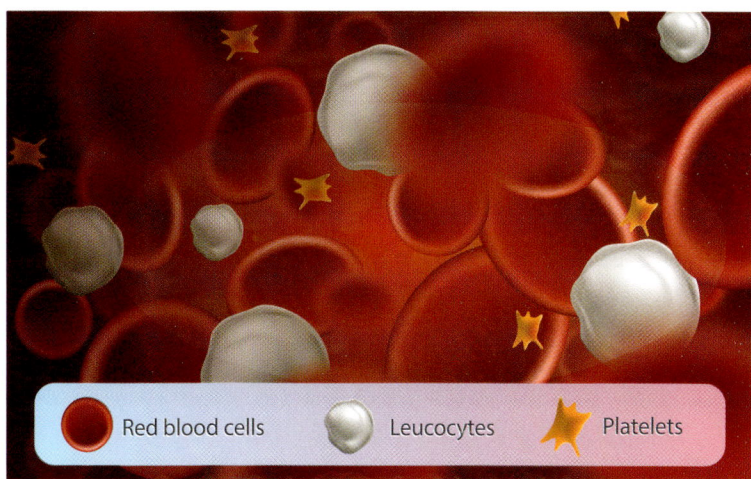

What Do Platelets Do?

In their short lives, platelets do a lot of things. In the blood, they circulate at the edges, near the walls of the veins and arteries. Because of this, they are the first to spot a hole or tear in the vein and can act immediately. The inner wall of a blood vessel is non-sticky (like a Teflon-coated pan), but the rest of our tissues are not. So, in a wound, platelets stick immediately and start the clotting process.

Platelets have other jobs too, in healing inflammation, in the development of the lymph vessels and in helping the liver regenerate.

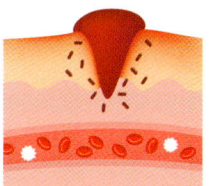 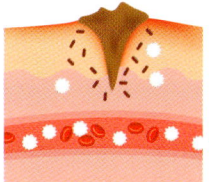 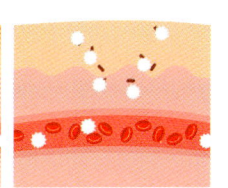

▲ After platelets seal a wound, new cells begin to grow

▲ The body stores extra platelets in the spleen, to prepare for emergencies

Platelet Count

A litre of blood in a normal person should have between 150 and 400 billion platelets. But because of diseases like dengue or thalassemia, one may not have enough platelets. If a person's platelet count is below 50 billion platelets per litre (ppl), one is at a serious risk of bleeding to death. On the other hand, if one has more than 400 ppl, one may get thrombosis.

Thrombosis

Thrombosis is a disorder of the body that causes clot formation inside the arteries and veins, because of which the flow of blood to organs gets choked, leading to organ failure. Thrombosis may be caused due to damage to the spleen, anaemia (too few RBCs) or cancer, or because the body makes too many platelets or too much fibrinogen.

In Real Life

Unlike a blood donation where your blood type has to be matched to the receiver's, you can donate platelets to anybody. Today, doctors realise that in most cases where a blood transfusion is required, giving only plasma or platelets is sufficient.

▼ A thrombus stops blood flow, starving the tissue around it of oxygen

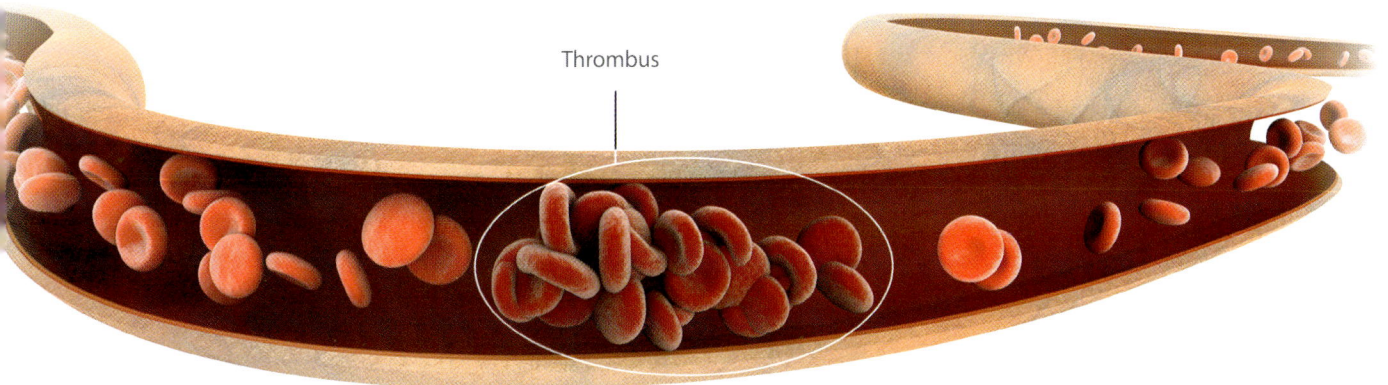

Thrombus

Keeping Our Gut and Lungs Safe

After our skin, our digestive system and our respiratory system interact with the environment the most. Our immune system works in special ways to keep the organ systems safe. Just as countries have a border, that is often fenced, the intestines and lungs have a strong wall called the epithelium. It also performs other functions like absorbing digested food in the intestine and oxygen in the lungs that need it to be really thin. Yet it must also form a stiff wall that prevents pathogens from the food or air from getting into the body. It does this by making sure that there are no gaps between cells.

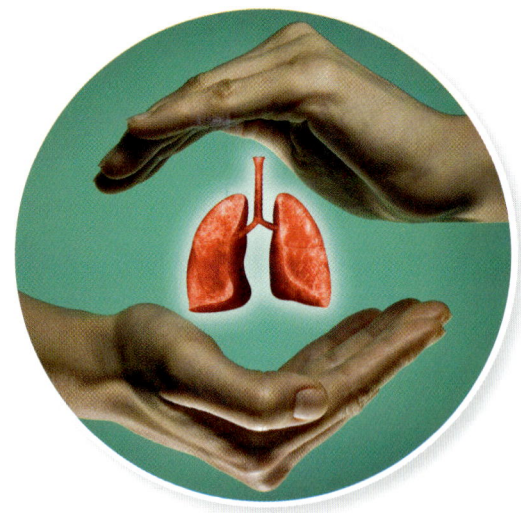

▲ The immune system keeps our lungs healthy and free of sickness

Epithelial Defences

The epithelium of the lungs has tiny hair called cilia that detect pathogens and alert the immune system. In the intestine, epithelia can sense harmful chemicals made by germs. In turn, they make cytokines and interleukins that alert the fighting cells of the immune system. *(see pp 20-21)*

The epithelia are also coated with a sticky, jelly-like material called **mucus**. This traps all foreign things and moves them to the digestive system. When you have a runny nose, your body makes a lot more mucus, which ends up coming out of your nose!

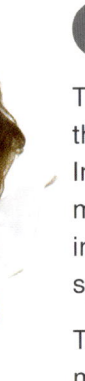

◄ Sneezing throws out germs that irritates the nose's epithelium

💡 Isn't It Amazing!

Lysozyme is found in egg whites and keeps the growing chick safe.

► Lysozyme is present in the saliva

Lysozyme: The Killer Enzyme

Lysozyme is the enzyme that is found in our saliva and in our tears. This very powerful enzyme digests the cell wall of bacteria, which makes them die. When mum kisses you, the lysozyme in her saliva attacks the bacteria on your skin. Perhaps that is why they say 'a mother's kiss heals sores'.

The Forts of Our Body

Just as armies built forts near borders inhabited by soldiers who would be ready to face an attack, our body too has tiny forts called MALTs associated with the lungs, nose, intestines and stomach. These have a large number of immune cells (T-cells, B-cells and macrophages) waiting in them, ready to attack any pathogen.

Our Microscopic Allies

Did you know that we have more bacteria living inside our intestines than we have cells in our entire body? These bacteria get into our system just after birth and live inside us throughout our lives. But do not worry, they are our friends, not our enemies. Together, they are called **gut microflora**.

Gut Microflora

Gut microflora perform a lot of different functions for the body. They crowd the surface of the intestines, so disease-causing bacteria do not get a place to settle down and start the infection. They make biochemical weapons that kill other bacteria. These are called bacterio-toxins. They also help to train the immune system when we are young, to recognise antigens and to distinguish good bacteria from the bad ones. They prevent us from contracting illnesses like diarrhoea.

Other bacteria live on our skin. They help themselves to the nutrients they can get from dandruff and sweat and make sure pathogens do not get to them. They turn them into smelly things, which is what gives you bad body odour, especially under the armpits. Showering regularly keeps them away.

▲ Bacteria in the large intestine finish up digestion

▶ The intestine is home to good bacteria that keep bad ones away

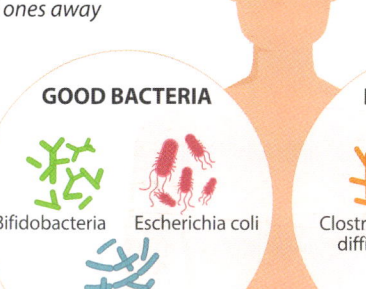
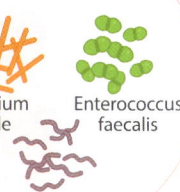

Incredible Individuals

Many cultures throughout the world eat a lot of fermented food. Fermentation is a process by which bacteria break down hard-to-digest things in food. Elie Metchnikoff was a famous scientist who noted that Bulgarian villagers ate a lot of yogurt and lived long lives. He soon found out that it was because yogurt had a bacteria called Lactobacilli in abundance. When you eat yogurt, these bacteria start living in your intestine, and prevent harmful bacteria from getting a chance to grow.

▲ Bulgarian villagers are known to eat lots of yogurt

Isn't It Amazing!

Did you know that a bacterium called Escherichia coli or E. coli inhabits the human intestine? This bacterium has helped us study how diseases are caused, how the body fights diseases and how we can develop drugs against them. It also makes Vitamin K12, which our body cannot make for itself.

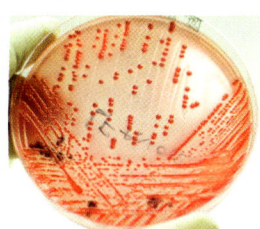

▲ Escherichia coli being grown in a petri dish

How Our Immune System Fights

If you have seen an action movie, it usually ends with the heroes saving the day. In the same way, in the case of a severe infection, the B-cells and T-cells take over the fight. Otherwise, they rest quietly in the lymph nodes. T-cells come in three types, based on how they act, while B-cells come in two.

Why Our Body Needs Immune Cells

Animals, like insects, did not have immune cells. But as mammals evolved to live longer lives, they needed a stronger immune system, so as to identify germs and be able to get rid of them.

B-cells and T-cells act much faster than phagocytic cells and neutralise the enemy. That is, they make it impossible for germs to hide or defend themselves, so that the phagocytes can then eat them up. They also have a lot of chemical weapons that other cells do not have.

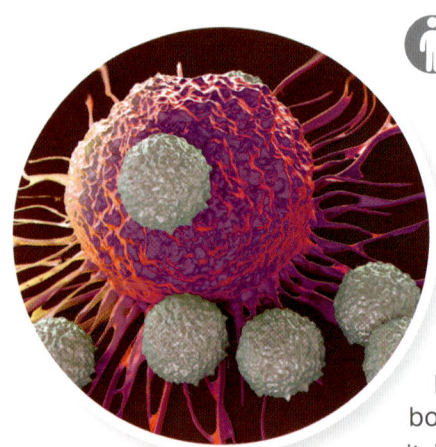
▲ *T-cell activation by phagocytes*

Killer T-cells

Killer T-cells are like assassins. Once they know their enemy, they kill it directly. Killer T-cells are called by phagocytic cells that have swallowed infected cells. If the antigen presented by the cell matches the record that the T-cell has, it immediately launches chemical weapons called granzymes and perforins. These invade the infected cell, killing both the cells and the pathogens that infected it. This is the immune system's way of getting at viruses that hide inside cells.

Lymph nodes

Appendix

Bone marrow

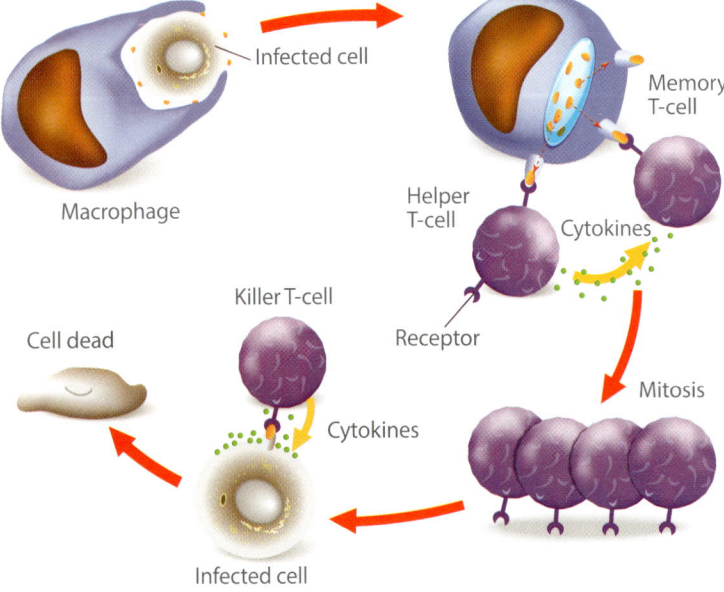
▲ *The diagram shows how the helper T-cells work*

Helper T-cells

Helper T-cells are cells that do not fight but call other T-cells and B-cells to fight. Once a T-cell has recognised the antigen, it puts out a kind of biochemical called an interleukin, that acts like a military siren. When a killer T-cell or a B-cell finds these interleukins, it knows that it needs to get ready for the fight. Such a cell is called an activated cell.

Memory T-cells

When a killer T-cell or helper T-cell is activated, it makes many copies or clones of itself. While most of the clones go off to fight harmful cells, some of them stay behind. They hang around in the lymph nodes and spleen until the pathogen comes back a second time. This time they become the helpers and start the fight all over again and also make copies for the next time.

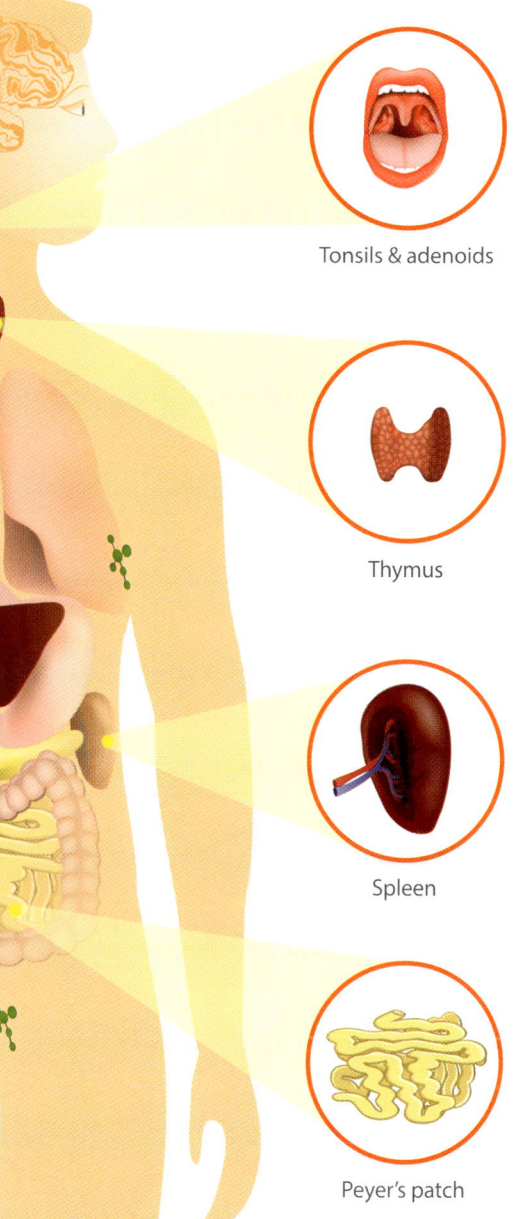

Isn't It Amazing!

WBCs travel in two ways. For most of the journey, they go with the pressure of flowing blood. Nearing the target, they stick to the blood vessel's walls. Here they put out pseudopodia (just like amoeba) and squeeze through the wall lining to enter the target tissue. The same pseudopodia also grab the bacteria.

▲ *The picture shows a sample of amoeba proteus*

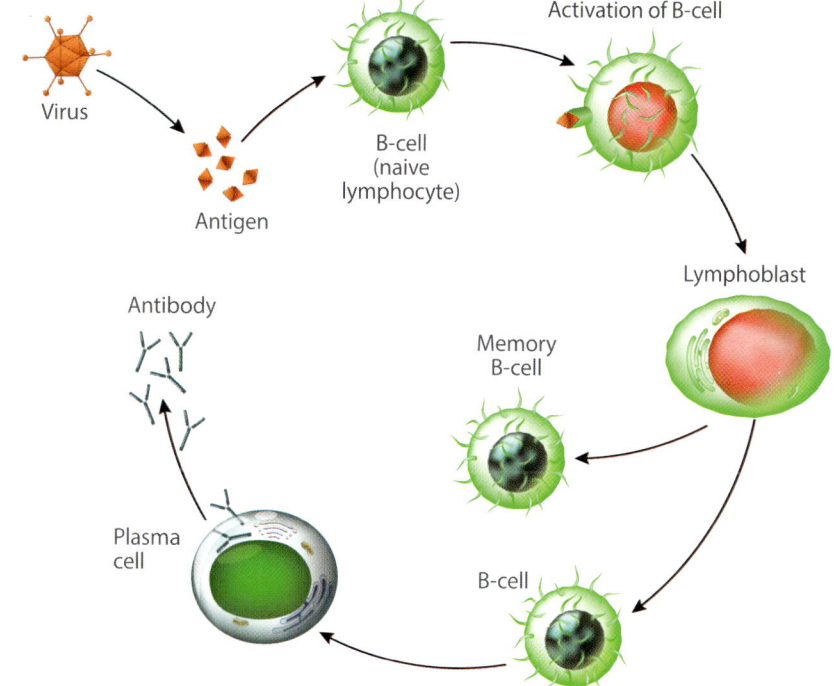

▲ *Different kinds of B-cells make different kinds of antibodies*

B-cells

B-cells are activated just like T-cells. But they do not kill by direct contact. Instead, they make antibodies and release them into the blood and lymph. When the antibodies find their matching antigen, they stick all over the pathogen and call the T-cells and macrophages to do the killing.

Like memory T-cells, there are memory B-cells too. Other activated B-cells turn into plasma cells, which are simply huge factories for making lots of antibodies. It is only the B-cells that match with antigens that turn into plasma cells. The other B-cells that do not match, stay quiet. This makes sure that only the infecting pathogen is destroyed, and the remaining tissue is safe.

Places where there are repeated infections, like the lungs and intestines, have a lot of B-cells and T-cells lying in wait for germs, in the tissues called MALT.

Our Immune System's Chemical Toolkit

Modern armies have all sorts of weapons and gadgets to fight a war—including radars and satellite phones, night vision goggles and jammers to block enemy communications. Our immune system also has gadgets like these, except that they are all chemical in nature. These tools give the immune system an incredible ability to act against any infection. They help the immune system increase or decrease the strength with which it responds, and also helps coordinate among all its cells. This is known as adaptability. They also prepare the rest of the body for fevers, and warn cells to look out for pathogens. During organ transplants, doctors give patients drugs called immuno-suppressants. These make sure that these immune chemicals do not attack the new organ.

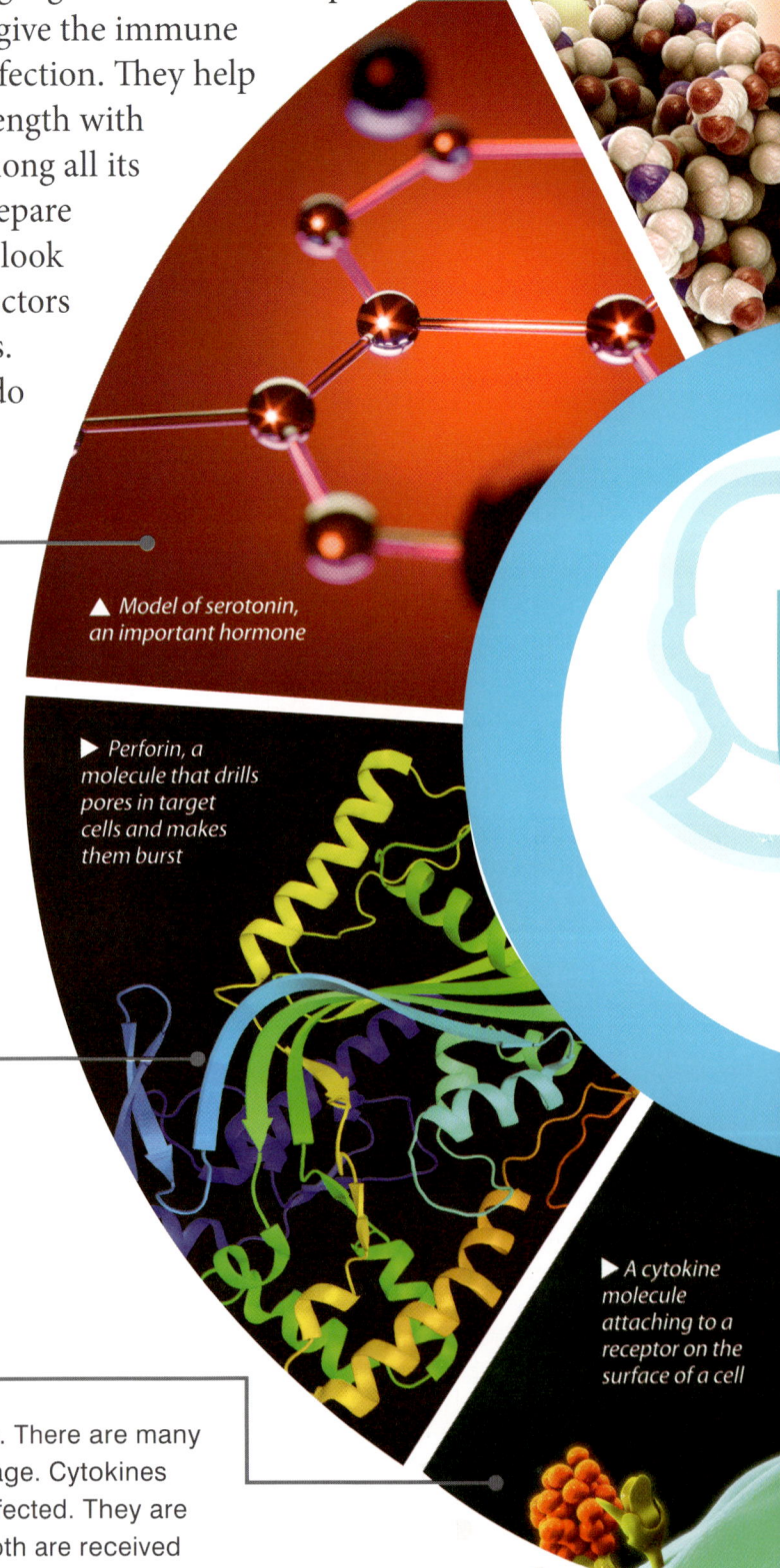

▲ Model of serotonin, an important hormone

▶ Perforin, a molecule that drills pores in target cells and makes them burst

▶ A cytokine molecule attaching to a receptor on the surface of a cell

Hormones

Many immune cells work in the same way as hormones in the body. Hormones are chemical messengers that travel through the blood and bind to proteins called receptors, on the surface of the cells.

If a receptor is a lock, a hormone is like the key that opens it. The same key can open different locks, i.e. the same hormone can interact with different kinds of receptors on different cells. Some hormones signal immune cells to stop being active, while other hormones make inactive immune cells active.

Granzymes & Perforins

These are enzymes that are stored in the granules of natural killer cells and also killer T-cells. When released, the perforins drill holes in the membranes of infected cells, causing them to burst. The granzymes (enzymes from the granules) then digest all the material.

Cytokines & Interleukins

These are the messenger proteins of the immune system. There are many kinds of cytokines, each of which carries a special message. Cytokines can be made by most cells of the body, but only when infected. They are also made by macrophages that have found antigens. Both are received by T-cells and B-cells that then get activated to do their jobs.

Interleukins are cytokines that are used by B-cells and T-cells to talk to each other. They are mostly made by helper T-cells.

HUMAN BODY | IMMUNE SYSTEM & COMMON DISEASES | 21

Interferons

These are messenger proteins that are released by the cells infected by viruses. They communicate to the immune system to send killer cells and macrophages to finish them off.

▼ Model of an anti-virus interferon.

Histamine

This little compound is the body's alarm siren. It is a messenger chemical, but different cells read it differently. Histamine is involved in blood clotting, increasing heartbeat (making the blood flow faster) and widening blood vessels among other things. It shrinks your lungs so you do not breathe in germs. However, too much histamine in the body causes an excessive allergic reaction, called anaphylactic shock.

◀ Histamines being released from an immune cell

Antibodies

These are the body's wonder weapons, and are made by activated B-cells. The medical term for them is **immunoglobulin**, Ig for short. They can be of the following five types:

IgM: This is the antibody made by B-cells the first time there is an infection.

IgG: These antibodies are made the second time there is an infection. IgG is made in huge quantities and can finish off the pathogen very quickly.

IgA: This antibody is released into the mucus of the intestines, lungs and tears to fight pathogens before they enter the body.

IgE: This antibody is meant for allergic reactions, though it works like the rest.

IgD: This antibody stays on the surface of the cell to help it recognise the pathogen.

◀ Immunoglobulins are Y-shaped molecules. The arms attach to antigens and the stems recruit killer cells

In Real Life

Babies don't just get nutrition from their mother's milk but also immunity. Immunoglobulin A travels into the baby's stomach, where it protects the baby from many diseases. Doctors call this passive immunity.

▲ Feeding on mother's milk is important for immunity among all mammals

Our Soldiers Never Forget

Have you ever wondered why you never get some diseases twice? For example, if you got chicken pox once, you will never get it again. This is because the immune system remembers all the pathogens that it has encountered. How does it do so?

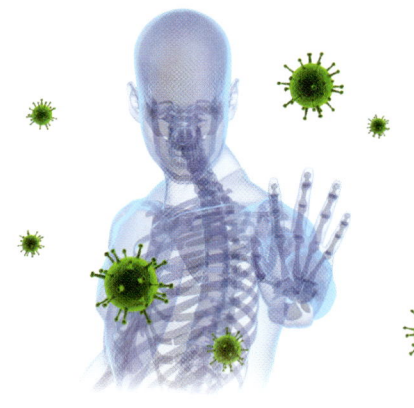

▶ A depiction of a healthy body fighting immune diseases

Memory

Whenever there is an infection, you know that the phagocytic cells eat up the pathogen and display bits of it on their surface. Thousands of B-cells and T-cells try to see whether they can match this antigen. This is done using a protein called a receptor, and each cell has a different one. The cell whose receptor matches becomes activated.

This activated cell will make thousands of cells like itself. Most of these cells will join the fight against the pathogen. But a few will remain in the lymph nodes, doing nothing. This is because their job is to wait for the next time the same pathogen attacks. Scientists call them memory cells.

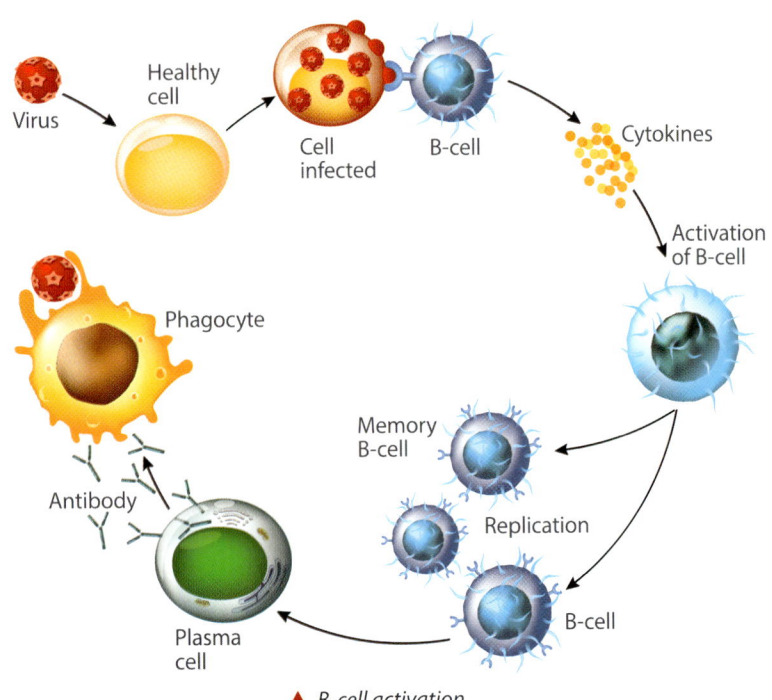

▲ B-cell activation

In Real Life

Our body's soldiers remember their targets through their receptors, so they have a large database of these receptors. Something like this is used by police everywhere—when they collect the fingerprints of people.

▲ The immune system matches antigens to pathogens, like police match fingerprints

 Making up Memories

The immune system responds best to a second infection by the same pathogen—but what if the first infection was fatal? When scientists found out this, they thought to themselves, what if there was a way to teach the memory of some common diseases to the immune system, so that when a real infection happened, it was fully ready for the fight. This is the thought behind vaccination. When you receive a vaccine, your body is administered with the disease–causing pathogen in a weakened state. This trains the body's immune system to fight a disease that it has not previously suffered. Thus, vaccines are meant to prevent disease.

◀ Vaccination helps create an artificial 'memory' of an infection, so that the immune system can respond faster when there's a real one

Why We Get Allergies

Some of us are allergic to dust, some to pollen and some even to nuts. All of these are called allergens. But why do we react to them, even though none of these cause any diseases?

▲ You can take tests to find out exactly what you are allergic to. People can be allergic to food additives, animal fur, pollen, etc

▼ Sneezing is a typical allergic reaction caused by inhaling allergens

Perceiving Danger

Our immune system really cannot make out whether anything foreign in our body causes diseases. However, it knows that all foreign bodies have to be destroyed. This trick works against germs. So, it makes antibodies against bacteria and interferons against viruses. But the body still does not know how it must deal with pollens and dust particles.

If You Can't Beat It, Overreact

Anything foreign in the body is seen off either by the phagocytes, or by the T-cells and B-cells. But many allergens still remain in the body. The immune system mounts a bigger response. It produces a lot of histamine, making the blood flow faster. The site of allergy becomes red and swollen. It makes a lot of IgE antibodies, which call in more killer cells. This leads to tissue damage, causing the rashes and welts that you see. Sadly, there is no true cure for allergy, except finding out what causes the allergy, and then trying your best to avoid it all of your life.

Asthma

Asthma is a kind of allergy caused by dust, pollen, smog and other things in the air. Whenever the allergen enters the lungs, it triggers the lymph nodes present there. A huge amount of histamine is produced and the lungs shrink, making it difficult to breathe.

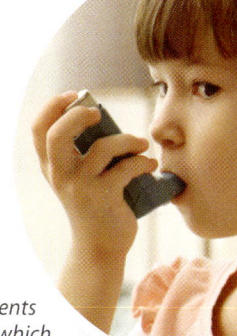

▶ Asthma patients use an inhaler, which contains a drug that makes the lungs expand again

Fighting Cancer

Every cell in our body undergoes wear and tear, which is not unusual. However, sometimes it so happens that the cell stops responding to the body's signals. This could be due to various factors such as infection by a virus, exposure to chemicals or UV light, etc. Under such a situation, the cells starts to function like a pathogen, and begins to multiply on its own. This uncontrolled multiplication leads to cancer.

As we evolved to live longer lives, the risk that we would get cancer also increased. Some scientists suggest that our complex immune system also evolved alongside to find and destroy cancers. Today, as vaccines and medicines have reduced the trouble caused by germs, cancer is becoming the biggest cause of death due to disease.

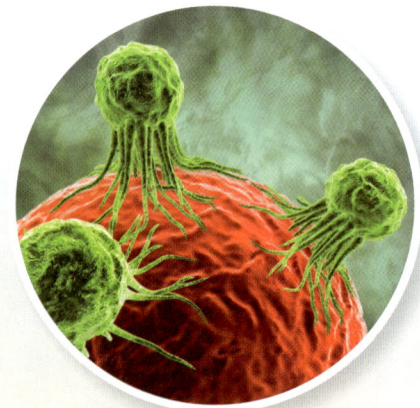

Spies Who Spot Cancer

All cells in our body have little proteins on their surface that act like ID cards. When we are inside our mother's womb, the immune system learns to not attack any cells that show these ID proteins. When a cell becomes cancerous, it stops showing these proteins. The neighbouring cells sense this and warn the immune system. The immune system in turn sends natural killer cells to the site to destroy the cancer cells.

◀ When the immune system loses, cancer cells multiply

◀ Meditation and some quiet time are said to be helpful to fight diseases

What Happens Next

Once a cell has become cancerous, it undergoes mutation of its DNA. It stops showing the self-ID antigens. The immune system then learns to recognise new antigens from the cancer cells and new T-cells and B-cells take up the fight. Some cancer cells die, but some mutate again, so that the antigens disappear. The immune system needs to start all over again. If the immune system wins, the cancer stops growing, and the lump of cells is called a benign tumour.

In Real Life

▲ An example of healthy food

Does eating healthy food like fruits and green vegetables help us fight cancer? Healthy food generally helps the immune system, however, scientists are still working on finding a direct link between a healthy diet and the suppression of cancer.

When Our Soldiers Turn Against Us

You have seen how the immune system reacts when it cannot overcome an allergy. Sometimes, this goes so far that the immune system loses its ability to differentiate the body's own cells from a foreign agent. Then the body begins to attack its own cells, causing an autoimmune disease.

This may happen because there is a genetic defect in the immune system, or because the antigens made from a pathogen may be very similar to one of the body's self-ID, which confuses the immune system. But in many autoimmune diseases, we do not know the cause. Luckily, very few of us will ever get them.

Major Autoimmune Diseases

Over 80 **autoimmune diseases** are known. Some of them are listed below.

Celiac disease
This happens when the immune system attacks the small intestine, causing indigestion, diarrhoea and pain.

Autoimmune Diabetes
If the immune system attacks the pancreas, it kills the cells that make insulin.

Rheumatic Fever
An infection by Streptococcus bacteria may cause this fever, because the antigens made from bacteria are very similar to proteins found in the valves of the heart.

Lupus Erythematosus
This is a very serious disease affecting many tissues of the body as the immune system attacks many proteins.

Myasthenia Gravis
The immune system attacks the meeting points of nerves and muscles, causing terrible weakness.

Rheumatoid arthritis
The immune system attacks the bone joints, causing pain all the time.

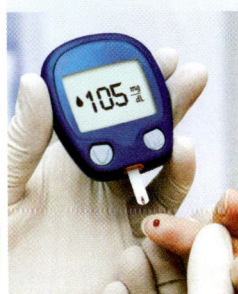
▲ Celiac disease causes poor digestion

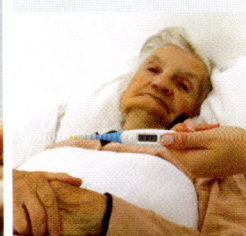
▲ The picture shows a blood sugar test for diabetes

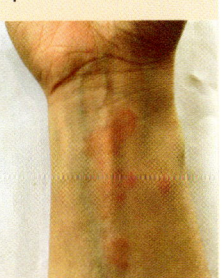
▲ Rheumatic fever causes frequent fever and pain

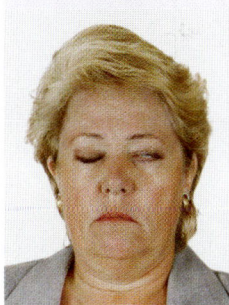
▲ Red blotches on the skin suggest lupus

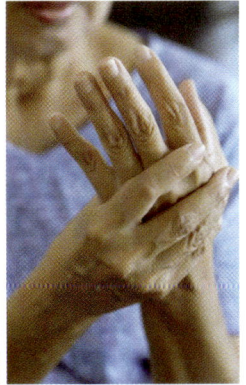
▲ Myasthenia gravis is a disease that leads to slow muscle loss

▲ Rheumatoid arthritis, showing the bending of joints

Blood-Brain Barrier

The brain is not directly nourished by blood or lymph. Hence, the immune system has never seen brain cells, nor learned to see them as part of the self. If there is an injury to the brain, and blood enters it, your immune system will attack it like it's a foreign body.

In Real Life

If you are someone who catches too many infections, you have a good chance of not getting autoimmune diseases later in life. This may be because the immune system is better trained to make out self and foreign antigens after it suffers from many infections.

▲ Playing in the mud exposes you to many pathogens, and helps the immune system learn better

Fighting Common Diseases

Our body fights diseases in many ways which help slow down pathogens and speed up the immune system. Even though it is not a part of the immune system, the brain plays a very important role too, as it communicates to the other organs to perform their functions. A part of the brain called the hypothalamus, is responsible for controlling body temperature, blood pressure, hunger and thirst. It works closely with the pituitary gland, which in turn controls other glands that make hormones. It is these hormones that communicate with other organs involved in performing functions such as storing iron, sneezing, making muscles contract, etc.

▼ *Fever causes fatigue, making the body want to rest so it can save the energy needed by the immune system*

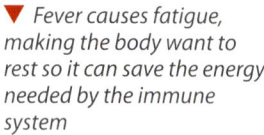

Fever

Most infectious bacteria and viruses do best when the temperature of our body is 37° C (98.6 °F). The brain tells all our tissues to raise their temperature. Bacteria and viruses are then made to feel the heat, literally! Fever happens in many diseases like typhoid, malaria, dengue, anthrax and Ebola among others.

Diarrhoea

Our body has ways to eliminate pathogens so that they don't harm us or make us ill. The intestine has many sensor cells that can find germs and toxins. These tell the autonomic nervous system and it immediately tells the intestine's muscles to contract and push the infected food out, along with the invaders. Doctors call this **diarrhoea**.

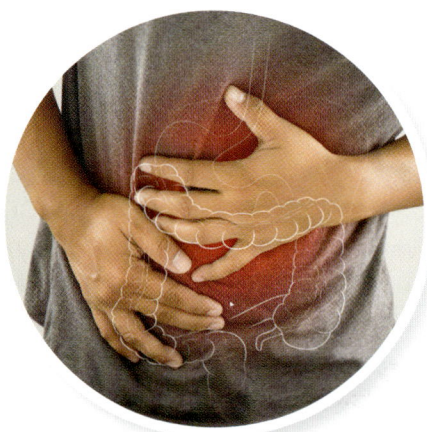

▲ *Diarrhoea cleans out the intestine, but without good hygiene, there can be other infections*

▼ *A young child with a runny nose*

Rhinorrhoea

Like the intestines, the nose has hair that can find out if something other than air has entered the respiratory system. They tell the brain and it causes sneezing. The lungs trap pathogens in their mucus, and then push the mucus out of the throat. This causes a runny nose (**rhinorrhoea**). This is our body's main way of fighting colds.

HUMAN BODY — IMMUNE SYSTEM & COMMON DISEASES

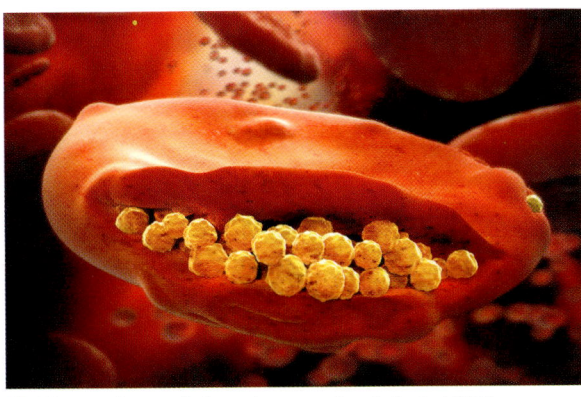
▲ Plasmodium cells bursting out of an infected RBC

Malaria

Malaria is a serious disease and the body has a tough time fighting it. This is because the pathogen that causes malaria, Plasmodium vivax, gets inside the RBCs, where it can escape the soldiers of the immune system. It multiplies there and breaks out of the RBCs, when the immune system catches it and triggers fever. But these pathogens get into other RBCs, this time causing chills in the body. Thus, you see many cycles of fever and chills.

In Real Life

The same allergen makes your immune system respond faster and stronger each time. In some cases though, it may lead to shock called anaphylaxis.

Hiding Iron

Bacteria need iron to survive and multiply. So, our body makes sure that they do not get it. It pulls out iron from the blood and hides it in the tissues, till the bacteria have been eliminated.

HIV/AIDS

HIV is the Human Immuno-deficiency Virus. Like the malaria bug, it hides in cells. But it is deadly because the cells it hides in are the very cells of the immune system! During an HIV infection, the virus destroys many WBCs, dangerously weakening the immune system. If it becomes severe, it causes AIDS—Acquired Immuno-Deficiency Syndrome. Patients with AIDS easily get other dangerous diseases like tuberculosis and malaria.

Today, however, we have drugs that fight HIV, called antiretrovirals. But what we need most is to help patients with HIV and treat them like anyone else with a disease. Sadly, many people avoid them because of ignorance.

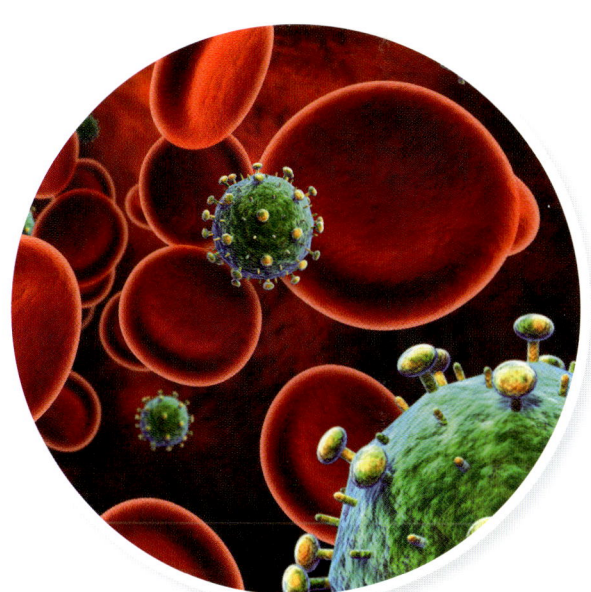
▲ HIV cells spread from one WBC to another through blood

Drink, Drink, Drink

You may have heard the old proverb—*starve the fever, feed the cold*. But is it true? Scientific studies have shown that you should in fact 'feed the fever, feed the cold'. For a cold this is fine—many colds run for over a week and your immune system needs the energy to keep fighting. During fever, which usually lasts for a day or two, you may not feel like eating. But your body's temperature rises, and you need more calories to keep up energy. Also, fever makes your body lose water and electrolytes, so you need to keep them up, even though you might not feel like it. The best thing to do, whether you have a cold, or a fever is to wrap up in warm clothes and drink lots of hot fluids—soup, milk or hot chocolate.

Isn't It Amazing!

Different animals have different body temperatures. For example, your pet dog has a natural body temperature of 38.9° C (102° F), which can feel feverish to us.

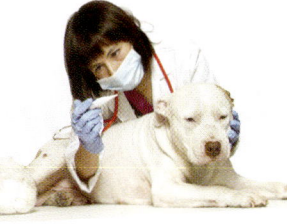
▶ A vet takes a dog's temperature

Vaccines: A Jab of Safety

When the vaccine enters the body, macrophages catch hold of it, and eat it up by phagocytosis. Some of the bits of the dead germ are shown on the outside of the cell *(see pp 11)*, and T-cells and B-cells try to recognise the antigen. Those who do, become activated. Most will fight the vaccine, but a few will turn into memory cells *(see pp 22)*. Your body was tricked into fighting a disease that wasn't there, but it left you vaccinated.

History of Vaccines

Edward Jenner (1749–1823) was the first to discover that having one disease can save you from others. He saw that the people in his village who got a disease called cowpox, did not get the much deadlier smallpox. Cowpox leaves little sores on the skin, and if you scrape material from these sores and inject them into healthy people, they too become immune. His discovery became a revolution in Europe: in 1811, Emperor Napoleon of France had his entire army vaccinated!

After Jenner, Louis Pasteur in France and Robert Koch in Germany continued to do a lot of research and developed a large number of vaccines—against rabies, anthrax, cholera, and many other diseases. Pasteur's students Calmette and Guerin developed a vaccine against tuberculosis, and Dr Robert Salk of Canada developed one against polio. Most vaccines have to be injected, but polio is given as drops in the mouth. You get polio by drinking contaminated water, and your body fights it in the intestine's MALT *(see pp 16)*.

Today, the government and doctors recommend that we give several vaccines to our children in order to help them become immune to many diseases.

▲ *A child getting a polio vaccine in Brazil*

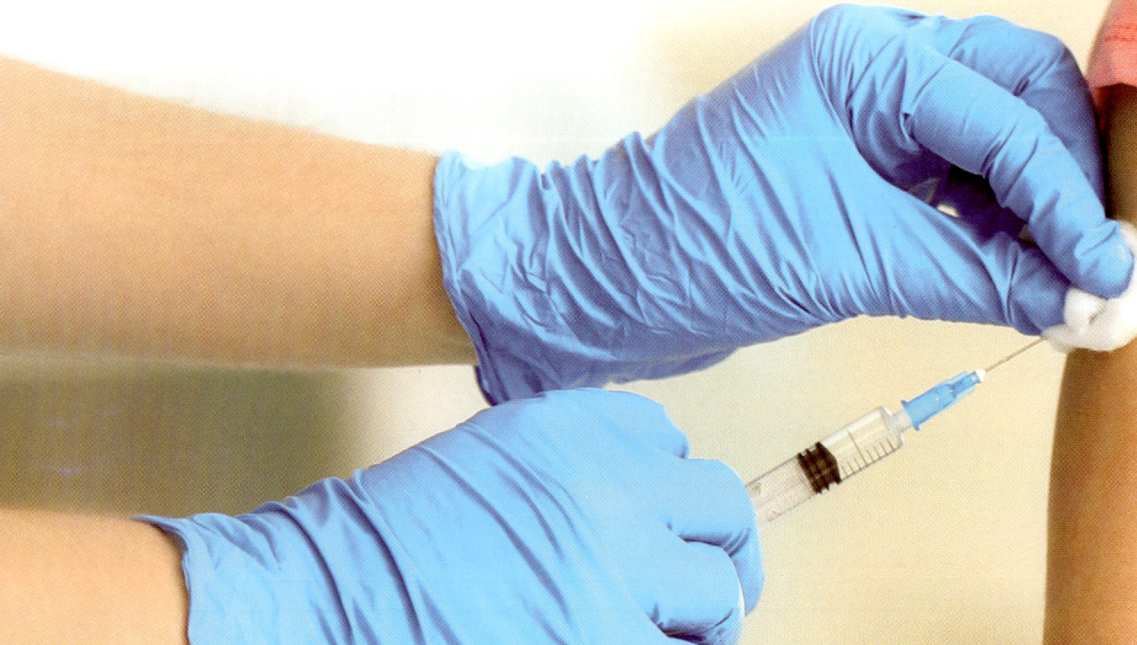

Isn't It Amazing!

Since the first vaccine came from cowpox, a disease that people get from handling cows, Louis Pasteur named this way of protecting our body after cows. The term vacca (in vaccination) is Latin for cow.

Cancer Vaccines

Today, researchers have found that some kinds of cancers can be prevented by making antibodies against them. It means we can make vaccines against such cancers. For now, we have vaccines against cervical cancer, but many more are being tested.

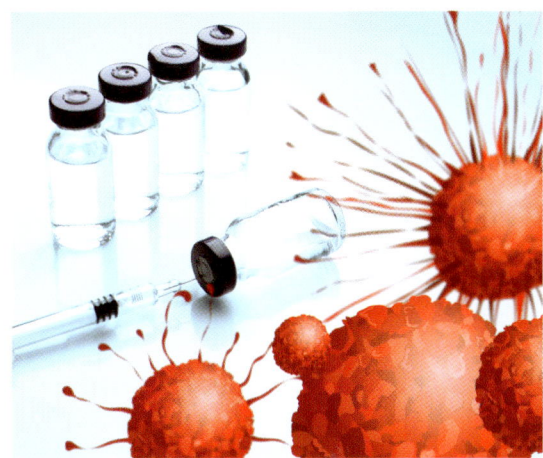

▶ Vaccines for many viral diseases are still being developed

▼ This is what an influenza virus looks like

Flu & HIV Vaccines

Influenza is a disease that is caused by many kinds of viruses. Because of this, we don't have a single vaccine that works against it. Also, many influenza viruses mutate, and their antigens keep changing, baffling the immune system. The HIV virus also does the same thing.

But there are different vaccines coming up against flu, and doctors say that you should get a jab every year to stay safe.

Incredible Individuals

Catherine the Great, the empress of Russia, wanted to introduce vaccination in her country. She made an offer: the first child who got vaccinated against smallpox, the Russian government would pay for their education and give them a pension. The first baby who got the vaccine was named Vaccinov!

▲ Catherine the Great, who introduced vaccination to Russia

Immunity in Plants and Animals

Do plants and animals have immune cells? Learning about how other creatures defend themselves from diseases can help us make better medicines to fight diseases.

How Plants Keep Themselves Safe

Plants get diseases too, from viruses, bacteria and fungi. Plant cells respond to these like our immune system does: by finding out what antigens are self, and what are foreign, through 'receptors' on their cell surface. If a plant cell detects a foreign body, it initiates phagocytosis.

◀ A plant with fungal disease

How Insects Stay Safe

Insects don't have an immune system like mammals, but they do have a lymph, and phagocytes that float around in it. Insects also make proteins called defensins. These proteins stop bacteria from growing.

How Bacteria Stay Safe

We read earlier that viruses infect bacteria too. But bacteria have a unique way of fighting them off. When a virus infects a bacterium (or any living thing), it injects its own DNA into the cell. This DNA makes copies of itself using the infected cell's resources. Bacteria have enzymes called Restriction Endonucleases (REs). These enzymes chop up the viral DNA into little bits.

Incredible Individuals

The Irish Famine (1845–49) happened when Ireland's main crop, potato, was infected by fungi. This disease, called late blight, kills the potato plant just as the potatoes are getting ready to eat. A million people died, and nearly 2 million emigrated to America. Among these were the Fitzgerald and Kennedy families, whose great-grandson John Fitzgerald Kennedy became president of the USA in 1961.

How Fungi Keep Themselves (and Us) Safe

Fungi live in places where they are regularly attacked by bacteria. They protect themselves by releasing chemicals into the environment, which prevent bacteria from growing. The first of these was discovered by Alexander Fleming, when he saw that a fungus called Penicillium had killed his bacterial cultures. He soon found the chemical that was doing this and named it penicillin. Ever since then, scientists have discovered hundreds of such chemicals from fungi, which we together call **antibiotics**.

▶ Penicillium growing in a lab culture of bacteria

Helping Our Immune System

Healthy food keeps the body fit, and generally helps the immune system. Fighting illness needs a lot of energy. You also need a lot of vitamins and minerals to ensure that the immune system is healthy and is able to make enough of its messenger molecules and chemical weapons. But most of all, you need to exercise a lot to keep your heart and circulation system healthy, so there's enough oxygen for all cells of your body.

Eating Healthy

What the immune system needs most are Vitamins K and D. Vitamin K is a necessary part of the clotting process. Without it, blood would not clot, and you could bleed uncontrollably. Good sources of vitamin K are green leafy vegetables, cheese and eggs.

Vitamin D is necessary for T-cells to function correctly. Vitamin D is made in our skin in the sunlight, but you can also get it from fish and mushrooms.

Sleep and Exercise

Lack of sleep or a lot of stress in the body causes the production of steroid hormones, which reduce immunity. On the other hand, exercise boosts immunity. It keeps up healthy circulation of blood (so WBCs can travel faster) and also reduces stress hormones. So, go out and play a lot!

◀ Young children should be encouraged to play outside so that they can make friends and get some exercise

◀ Eating vegetables rich in vitamins is as necessary for your body as exercising

Hormones

Some steroid hormones in our bodies, like testosterone and cortisol, suppress the immune system. The body makes more of them when the immune system has fought off the pathogen, and energy is needed for other things. In autoimmune disease, these hormones are used to protect the body from being attacked by its own immune cells.

In Real Life

Did you know that listening to music for 50 minutes every day can help boost your immunity? This is because music helps calm the mind and reduces stress in the body. So, when you're studying or travelling, listening to music is a good idea!

◀ Listening to music is good for your mind and your body

Word Check

Allergens: They are the things that cause allergies.

Antibiotics: They are the chemicals made by fungi to protect themselves from bacteria.

Antibodies: These are proteins made by the B-cells that stick to specific antigens and get the rest of the immune system to destroy them.

Antigens: They are parts of foreign bodies used by the immune system to recognise an infection/allergy and destroy it.

Autoimmune disease: It is a kind of disease in which our immune system attacks cells of our own body.

Bacteriophage: It is a virus that infects bacteria.

Complement pathway: It is the number of proteins that react with each other to make the blood clot in case of an injury.

Dendritic Cells: They are the phagocytic cells that enter tissues from the blood. They swallow pathogens and present antigens to T-cells and B-cells.

Dermis: It is the inner layer of the skin, made of live cells, hair follicles and sebaceous glands.

Diarrhoea: It is the defence against infection which makes the intestines rapidly throw out bad food.

Epidermis: It is the outer layer of skin that acts like a waterproof wall against pathogens and allergens.

Fibrin: It is a protein in the blood that makes tiny fibres that seal a wound during clotting.

Gut Microflora: They are the bacteria that live in our large intestines, which make vitamins and keep bad bacteria from infecting us.

Hair Follicles: They are the cells in the dermis which give rise to hair.

Helminths: They are a class of microscopic worms, some of which infect us.

Histamines: They are the biochemicals which trigger an inflammation or allergy in response to an infection or allergen.

Hypodermis: It is the third layer of the skin. It is a deeper subcutaneous tissue made up of fat and connective tissue.

Immunoglobulin: It is the medical term for antibodies.

Inflammation: It is the body's reaction to insect bites, or some infections marked by redness and pain in the affected part of the body.

Keratin: It is the protein that makes hair and nails.

Langerhans Cells: They are the phagocytic cells in the skin.

Lymph Nodes: They are the glands that filter lymph and act as resting and training centres for WBCs.

Lymphatic System: It is the body's second circulatory system after blood, which drains tissues and hosts WBCs.

Lysosomes: They are the bags of enzymes inside each human cell that contain germ-destroying enzymes.

Macrophages: They are the WBCs that spot and kill harmful pathogens.

Melanin: It is the dark pigment that gives our skin its colour and keeps us safe from UV rays.

Mucus: It is the slime that covers the epithelium and keeps germs from getting into the body.

Natural Killer Cells: They are the WBCs full of granzymes and perforins that kill infected cells.

Pathogens: They are the germs that attack us, like bacteria, fungi, viruses, protozoa and helminths.

Phagosome: It is a sac inside a cell which contains the swallowed pathogen. It will merge with a lysosome.

Rhinorrhoea: It is a defence against infection which makes the lungs rapidly throw out mucus from the nose, along with germs trapped in it.

Sebaceous glands: They are the glands in the skin that make sebum.

Sebum: It is the oil made by the skin that keeps our body waterproof.

Sweat Glands: They are the glands in the skin that make sweat. Sweat evaporates from the skin and keeps us cool.